Discover The Winner Within You

An instant discovery can
bring you personal power,
real wealth, and great influence.

DISCOVER THE WINNER WITHIN YOU

Moody Adams

Scriptures from the King James Bible with obsolete words
updated except when contained within an author's quote

A PUBLICATION OF *THE*
MOODY ADAMS EVANGELISTIC ASSOCIATION

To Miss Betty

The Scotch girl
who has been
the story of my life,
the mother of my children, and
the manager of my ministry,
for 51 good years,
with the best ones
yet to come.

CONTENTS

1. The Great Discovery — 10
2. The Winner's Guide — 15
3. The Truth That Transformed the Apostles — 18
4. They Made the Discovery — 21
5. Three Stages of Life's Great Discovery — 25
6. A 4,000-Year-Old-Mystery Revealed — 28
7. You are Complete in Christ — 31
8. Christ Meets all Needs — 33
9. The Secret of the Substitute — 35
10. Soar Higher in Life — 38
11. Experience the Exciting Exchanged Life — 40
12. The Winner's Home — 43
13. Triumph Through a Powerful Purpose — 45
14. Knowing Heaven is on Your Side — 48
15. Experience the Most Mysterious Miracle — 50
16. Escape the Loser's Snare — 52
17. Turn Your Defeats Into Victories — 55
18. Seize This Fantastic Study in Success — 58
19. Master the Rewarding Riddle of Receptivity — 60
20. The Key to the Mysteries of our Universe — 63
21. God Gives, we Simply Receive — 66
22. The Mystery of the Life of Jesus Christ — 69
23. Christ Motivates us From Within — 72
24. Everything Good is Received From God — 75
25. Start Over With a New Self-image — 79

26. The Benefits of a Decaying Body   82
27. Get Rid of Guilt Forever   86
28. Win the Reward of Wisdom   89
29. The Winner's Wealth   93
30. The True Riches   98
31. Live In Need of Nothing   103
32. Let the Submarine's Secret Work for You   106
33. Become a Champion of Persevering Patience   110
34. Stop Struggling and Start Succeeding   112
35. The Power to Succeed   116
36. When Your Strength Ends, God's Begins   119
37. Nuclear Power was Always Here   122
38. Free Your Life from Worry   124
39. How to Overcome Your Opposition   126
40. Surviving a Broken Heart   129
41. Succeed through Self-control   131
42. The way to win Over Temptation   134
43. Making Sure You Will Never Give Up   136
44. Become a Positive Influence   140
45. More Than a Conqueror   143
46. Possessing Earth's Most Powerful Force   146
47. Showing Others How to Win   152
48. Overcome Your Past Defeats   156
49. Experience Unspeakable Joy   159
50. Joy is the Echo of God's Life in Man's Soul   162
51. Win Over Horrible Handicaps   165
52. Satisfaction That Never Ends   168
53. Experience Endless Enthusiasm   171
54. Winners Live in Another World   173
55. Face the Future With Unshakable Assurance   176
56. Start Your Winning Life Today   181

**CHAPTER
ONE**

THE GREAT DISCOVERY

"The mystery which hath been hid from ages and from generations, but now is made manifest . . . God would make known what is the riches of the glory of this mystery . . . which is Christ IN YOU" (Colossians 1:26, 27).

There is a great discovery awaiting you. Your moment can come. You can make a discovery of wealth so vast your life will never be the same again. It will transform you into a Winner for the ages.

In the mid-sixties I met a man who made a life-changing discovery. I had been invited to speak at Satellite Beach, Florida. My host knew that I enjoyed diving and he mentioned to me, "Moody, I have a friend that is a diver. I would like to introduce you to him. Perhaps the two of you can get together for some skin diving." I replied that I would enjoy it. Later, he introduced me to the tall, erect, athletic diver, a man in his forties named Bob Johnson. I immediately launched the conversation into the subject of diving: "Bob, I understand you are a diver." He replied, "Yes." His one-word reply made it obvious that Bob wasn't overly talkative.

I saw that any information I got out of this man would have to be drawn out. I probed, "Bob, do you dive to spear fish?" "No" was his typical one-word answer. I said, "Do you dive for the exercise?" Again he replied, "No," Getting a little desperate I said, "Well, Bob, what in the world do you dive for? To my surprise he replied, "Treasure."

I laughed, thinking it rather amusing that a grown man would still hold to the childish dream of discovering hidden treasures. I started kidding him: "Bob, I gave up any hopes of finding lost treasure when I was thirteen years old. Don't tell me that a man of your age is still groping around out in the water hoping to strike it rich." His reply was "Yes." It came soberly with a curious lack of even a smile. I asked, "Bob, did you ever find anything of any value?" "A couple of times," he replied.

"What was the most valuable find?" I asked him. Finally he started talking, "Well, we don't really know how much it's worth yet because we are not through bringing all of it up, but so far we have gotten about two million dollars from the wreckage of eleven Spanish ships off the coast!"

The greatest historical discovery of the century

I made the shocking discovery that I was talking to a man who was one of the great divers in the history of the world. Bob Johnson was a key member in the Real Eight Company that made what the National Geographic Society called the greatest historical discovery of this century. They found the wreckage of a treasure-laden Spanish armada off the coast of Florida.

Bob Johnson told me the story. In the eighteenth century, Spain sent an armada of ships over to the New World about every five years to bring back treasure. In 1715, seven ships made their way to Havana, Cuba, the gathering point for all treasures in the New World. A general, who was closely aligned with the king, made this particular voyage to assure the ship's speedy return. The treasure was urgently needed to save the king from pressing political problems.

Havana, Cuba was the gathering point for Spain's New World treasure. Pottery was brought from the Far East, carried across land where the Panama Canal now connects two oceans, and reloaded on ships for passage to Havana. Silver and gold was gathered from all over North and Central America and shipped there.

When the Spanish armada finished loading the eleven ships with treasure, the weather was very bad. The admiral decided sailing was too dangerous. But the general, concerned with his king's troubles at home, said, "We have to leave immediately." Quite an argument followed, but it so happened that the general outranked the admiral, and therefore they failed immediately.

The fleet never made it to Spain. A hurricane dashed the ships to pieces just below Cape Kennedy. On July 31, 1715, at 1:20 a.m., beaches of sand were turned into beaches of gold!

Many years later Bob Johnson would discover the wreckage of these Spanish ships. Bob said the amazing part of the entire discovery was the mystery of how this treasure could have gone undiscovered. Seven months out of the year, the ten feet of water was so clear anyone could easily see the cannons and sandstones that denoted a shipwreck. Yet men fished and swam so near great wealth and they never claimed a cent.

The treasure hunter's secret

I wondered how Bob discovered this treasure that had laid in the sand so long and been missed by so many. He explained to me, "Moody, treasure hunters do not go about their work in the way most people think. Virtually all treasure discoveries begin in some ancient, dusty book containing maps and stories of shipwrecks. Those who really want to find treasure spend most of their life studying these old maps and historical records."

Study your treasure map

You have access to ancient writings, thousands of years old, that point you to a far greater treasure than Bob Johnson found in the waters of the Atlantic. Among many other things the Bible is a treasure map pointing you to great hidden riches: "The mystery which hath been hid from ages and from generations, but now is made manifest . . . God would make known what is the riches of the glory of this mystery . . . which is Christ IN YOU" (Colossians 1:26, 27).

That is it! The treasures of unsurpassed wonder and value, Christ living inside your mortal body. Every man can receive Christ's Spirit into his heart. Once he does, he has the Great Winner living in him. Once he discovers this, he immediately possesses the riches of power, influence, success, everlasting joy, and far, far more.

My Daily Journal

On what date did you read this lesson ?__________

Study to show thyself approved unto God, a workman that needs not to be ashamed (2 Tim 2:15).

What Christ-like deed have you done?

____

____

Why do you call me Lord, Lord and not do the things that I say (Luke 6:46)?

Which temptations have you overcome?

____

____

Blessed is the man that endures temptation: for when he is tried, he shall receive the crown of life (James 1:12).

Which temptations have you yield to?

____

____

If we confess our sins, he is faithful and just to forgive us our sins, and to cleanse us from all unrighteousness (I John 1:9).

CHAPTER TWO

THE WINNER'S GUIDE

"The abiding indwelling of Jesus Christ in the heart of the believer is an experience more to be coveted than any other. It constitutes the crown and climax of the Christian life."
—Gregory Mantle

The Bible contains a marvelous map which shows you the way to winning. The masses of people see nothing in Jesus Christ but the sands of rituals and regulations. But there have been a few who have dug through the sand and discovered the gold. You can join them by trusting the guide of God.

God promised the prophet Isaiah, "And I will give thee the treasures . . . and hidden riches of secret places" (Isaiah 45:3). These treasures can be yours.

You can shout the song of David: "O Lord . . . you fill me with thy hid treasure" (Psalm 17:14). Four thousand years ago God first made the promise: "I will dwell IN THEM, and walk IN THEM" (Leviticus 26:12).

God came to earth
that He might live inside you

The purpose of Jesus entering history was that He might enter men! He said of His followers, "He . . . dwells in me, and I IN HIM" (John 6:56).

Christ said, "You shall know that I am in my Father and . . .IN YOU" (John 14:20).

Jesus promised His disciples, "I (will abide) IN YOU" (John 15:4).

Our Lord said of the true believer, "I (will abide) IN HIM" (John 15:5).

Christ said, "I (will dwell) IN THEM" (John 17:23).

Jesus declared God's name to men for the stated purpose that He might dwell "IN THEM" (John 17:26).

Christ was not content merely to instruct men or to set them an example. He is not only the "way and the truth," but also the "life."

My Daily Journal

On what date did you read this lesson ?________

Study to show thyself approved unto God, a workman that needs not to be ashamed (2 Tim 2:15).

What Christ-like deed have you done?

____

____

Why do you call me Lord, Lord and not do the things that I say (Luke 6:46)?

Which temptations have you overcome?

____

____

Blessed is the man that endures temptation: for when he is tried, he shall receive the crown of life (James 1:12).

Which temptations have you yield to?

____

____

If we confess our sins, he is faithful and just to forgive us our sins, and to cleanse us from all unrighteousness (I John 1:9).

CHAPTER
THREE

THE TRUTH THAT TRANSFORMED THE APOSTLES

*"The abiding indwelling of Jesus Christ
in the heart of the believer is an experience
more to be coveted than any other. It constitutes
the crown and climax of the Christian life. "
—Gregory Mantle*

The apostles were so transformed by their discovery they could not help but declare over and over the "riches of this mystery . . . Christ IN YOU."

"And if Christ be IN YOU, the body is dead because of sin" (Romans 8:10).

"Know you not . . . that Jesus Christ is IN YOU" (II Corinthians 13:5).

"Christ lives IN ME" (Galatians 2:20).

"It pleased God . . . to reveal His Son IN ME" (Galatians 1:15, 16).

"That Christ may dwell IN YOUR HEARTS by faith" (Ephesians 3:17).

"Christ IN YOU, the hope of glory" (Colossians

1:27).

"You have therefore RECEIVED Christ Jesus the Lord" (Colossians 2:6).

"Hereby know we that . . . he is IN US" (I John 4:13).

"Greater is he that is IN YOU, than he that is in the world" (I John 4:4).

"Christ is all, and IN ALL" (Colossians 3:11).

"Behold, I stand at the door, and knock: if any man hear my voice, and open the door, I will come IN TO HIM" (Revelations 3:20).

This imposing weight of scripture all points to the glorious mystery of Christ IN YOU.

Mankind's greatest experience

Gregory Mantle says this is treasure of victory to be pursued above all else on earth: "The abiding indwelling of Jesus Christ in the heart of the believer is an experience more to be coveted than any other. It constitutes the crown and climax of the Christian life. God not only pardons our guilt and saves us from its consequences; He not only forgives, saying: 'Go in peace and sin no more'; He not only gives us a new nature, one that loves to do right and hates to do wrong; He not only comes to our aid in temptation and trial, and interposes His strength and succor; but, above all this, He comes to live His own wonderful life in us in the Person of His Son Jesus Christ, and says to work out your own salvation with fear and trembling, 'for it is God who works in you both to will and to work, for His good pleasure'" (Philippians 2:12, 13).[1]

This was the truth that transformed the apostles, God was working in them to do His "good pleasure."

My Daily Journal

On what date did you read this lesson ?_________

Study to show thyself approved unto God, a workman that needs not to be ashamed (2 Tim 2:15).

What Christ-like deed have you done?

____

____

Why do you call me Lord, Lord and not do the things that I say (Luke 6:46)?

Which temptations have you overcome?

____

____

Blessed is the man that endures temptation: for when he is tried, he shall receive the crown of life (James 1:12).

Which temptations have you yield to?

____

____

If we confess our sins, he is faithful and just to forgive us our sins, and to cleanse us from all unrighteousness (I John 1:9).

CHAPTER
FOUR

THEY
MADE THE
DISCOVERY

*"There is only one life that wins; and that is the life
of Jesus Christ. Every man may have that life
and every man may live that life."
—Charles G. Trumbull*

Charles G. Trumbull discovered the Winner within him. This outstanding Christian statesman testifies, "There is only one life that wins; and that is the life of Jesus Christ. Every man may have that life and every man may live that life. I do not mean that every man may be Christ like; I mean something very much better than that. I do not mean that a man may always have Christ's help; I mean something better than that. I do not mean that a man may have power from Christ; I mean something very much better than power. And I do not mean that a man shall be merely saved from his sins and kept from sinning; I mean something better than even that victory . . . Christ Himself is better than any of His blessings; better than the power, or the victory, or the service, that He grants. Christ creates spiritual power, but Christ is better than power. He is God's best; He is God; and we may have this best: we may have Christ, yielding to Him in such completeness and abandonment of self that it is no longer we that live, but Christ lives in us."[2]

Maltbie Babcock made the discovery and no longer envied the disciples

Maltbie Babcock made the transforming discovery that Jesus Christ was living inside her body and exclaimed:

"I envy not the twelve;
Nearer to me is he,
The life he once lived here on earth
He lives again in me."

Norman Grubb discovered a whole man is really God in a man

Though it was great to read that Jesus had lived among His disciples, Mrs. Babcock discovered something far greater—that same Jesus was living inside her body.

Norman Grubb exclaimed, "This perfect Man shows us perfectly the hidden meaning of creation... the creature nothing but a container, the Creator living His own life in the creature . . . a whole man is really God in a man . . . There is no other life."

A. B. Simpson declared
"Christ to my heart has come"

A. B. Simpson discovered the beaches of gold and was transformed into a great author and missionary leader. He declared,

"This is my wonderful story,
Christ to my heart has come;
Jesus, the king of glory,
Finds in my heart a home."

Rufus McDaniel put this
to song when he wrote *Since Jesus Came*
Into My Heart

After Rufus McDaniel discovered the Winner within him, he started to sing:

"What a wonderful change
In my life has been wrought
Since Jesus came into my heart!
I have light in my soul
For which long I have sought,
Since Jesus came into my heart."

Alexander Maclaren declared
the indwelling of Christ is
a plain, literal fact

Dr. Alexander Maclaren, whose writings would shape future generations, declared, "Let me say in the plainest, simplest, strongest way I can, that the dwelling of Christ in the believing heart is to be regarded as being a plain, literal fact . . . It is not to be weakened down into any notion of participating in his likeness, following his example or the like. A dead Plato may so influence his followers, but that is not how a living Christ influences his disciples . . . . God means and wishes that Christ may continuously dwell in our hearts."

My Daily Journal

On what date did you read this lesson ?_________

Study to show thyself approved unto God, a workman that needs not to be ashamed (2 Tim 2:15).

What Christ-like deed have you done?

____

____

Why do you call me Lord, Lord and not do the things that I say (Luke 6:46)?

Which temptations have you overcome?

____

____

Blessed is the man that endures temptation: for when he is tried, he shall receive the crown of life (James 1:12).

Which temptations have you yield to?

____

____

If we confess our sins, he is faithful and just to forgive us our sins, and to cleanse us from all unrighteousness (I John 1:9).

THREE STAGES OF LIFE'S GREAT DISCOVERY

"Lord, Thy love at last has conquered;
Grant me now my supplication,
'None of Self and all of Thee."
—*Gregory Mantle*

Gregory Mantle wrote, "I very much question whether the change, from absolute selfishness to absolute selflessness, has ever been more effectively described than by Theodore Monod in his well-known hymn.

"The first verse describes Self enthroned as Sovereign:
'Oh! the bitter shame and sorrow,
That a time could ever be,
When I let the Savior's pity
Plead in vain, and proudly answered,
'All of Self and none of Thee.'

"The second verse describes the beginning of love's conquest, and the shaking of the dominion of

Self:
'Yet He found me; I beheld Him
Bleeding on the accursed tree:
Heard Him pray, 'Forgive them, Father,'
And my wistful heart said faintly,
'Some of Self and some of Thee.'

"The third verse describes the anxiety of Self to be retained as Prime Minister, if not as King:
'Day by day His tender mercy,
Healing, helping, full and free,
Sweet and strong, and ah! so patient,
Brought me lower, while I whispered,
'Less of Self, and more of Thee.'

"The last verse describes the complete subjugation of Self by the Christ of Calvary, and the enthronement of Jesus as King:
'Higher than the highest heavens,
Deeper than the deepest sea,
Lord, Thy love at last has conquered;
Grant me now my supplication,
'None of Self and all of Thee.'"[8]

My Daily Journal

On what date did you read this lesson ?______

Study to show thyself approved unto God, a workman that needs not to be ashamed (2 Tim 2:15).

What Christ-like deed have you done?

____

____

Why do you call me Lord, Lord and not do the things that I say (Luke 6:46)?

Which temptations have you overcome?

____

____

Blessed is the man that endures temptation: for when he is tried, he shall receive the crown of life (James 1:12).

Which temptations have you yield to?

____

____

If we confess our sins, he is faithful and just to forgive us our sins, and to cleanse us from all unrighteousness (I John 1:9).

**CHAPTER
SIX**

A 4,000-YEAR-OLD-
MYSTERY REVEALED

**"This is a matter that God delights to bring to us
with a new flash of understanding. Suddenly one
day we see that Christ is our life (Colossians 3-4).
That day everything is changed. There is a
day . . . when we see that Christ within us is our
life. That too alters our whole outlook ."**
—*Watchman Nee*

The expectation of the ages can be fulfilled in
your body. Paul explains that the ancient prophecies
have been fulfilled: "You are the temple of the living
God; as God hath said, 'I will dwell in them, and walk
in them; and I will be their God, and they shall be my
people'" (II Corinthians 6:16). Moses' prophecy
spoken thousands of years before in Leviticus 26:12
has been fulfilled. God has come to live inside men
and to walk in them. You can experience it! God can
live and walk in your body every day!

The promise given to the great patriarch Abraham
is now given to you. Galatians 3:14 says, "That the

blessing of Abraham might come unto Gentiles through Jesus Christ; that we might receive the promise of the spirit through faith." The promise that God gave Abraham was not merely a promise of forgiveness, but of the Spirit. He was promised an inner union with God through His Spirit. And today that same promise is given to you: "And because you are sons, God has sent forth the spirit of His Son into your hearts" (Galatians 4:6). The same God that brought Abraham great power and influence can live inside your body! The same God that transformed Abraham into a man of great power and influence can do the same for you!

My Daily Journal

On what date did you read this lesson ? _______

Study to show thyself approved unto God, a workman that needs not to be ashamed (2 Tim 2:15).

What Christ-like deed have you done?

____

____

Why do you call me Lord, Lord and not do the things that I say (Luke 6:46)?

Which temptations have you overcome?

____

____

Blessed is the man that endures temptation: for when he is tried, he shall receive the crown of life (James 1:12).

Which temptations have you yield to?

____

____

If we confess our sins, he is faithful and just to forgive us our sins, and to cleanse us from all unrighteousness (I John 1:9).

**CHAPTER
SEVEN**

YOU ARE "COMPLETE" IN CHRIST

All the fullness of God was in Jesus Christ and Jesus Christ is in you

The two greatest thoughts my mind has ever tried to comprehend are found in the book of Colossians. The first great teaching of this book is Colossians 2:9: "For in Him dwells all the fullness of the Godhead bodily." Think of it, all the fullness of the Godhead, all the fullness of the Creator and sustainer of the universe was embodied in Jesus Christ.

Then Colossians 1:27 adds, "To whom God would make known what is the riches of the glory of this mystery among the Gentiles; which is Christ in you, the hope of glory." Our minds are too small to comprehend it. But what a thrill to even consider this. All the fullness of God was in Jesus Christ and Jesus Christ is in you. Every believer has the life of God in his body! Because of this Paul can say, "And you are complete in Him" (Colossians 2:10). "Complete" means we lack nothing, we need nothing, we have all the golden treasures in our earthen vessels. Christ is the fullness of the Godhead and Christ is in us!

My Daily Journal

On what date did you read this lesson ?_________

Study to show thyself approved unto God, a workman that needs not to be ashamed (2 Tim 2:15).

What Christ-like deed have you done?

____

____

Why do you call me Lord, Lord and not do the things that I say (Luke 6:46)?

Which temptations have you overcome?

____

____

Blessed is the man that endures temptation: for when he is tried, he shall receive the crown of life (James 1:12).

Which temptations have you yield to?

____

____

If we confess our sins, he is faithful and just to forgive us our sins, and to cleanse us from all unrighteousness (I John 1:9).

CHAPTER
EIGHT

CHRIST MEETS ALL NEEDS

*"This is a matter that God delights
to bring to us with a new flash
of understanding. Suddenly one day
we see that Christ is our life"
—Watchman Nee*

Dr. A. B. Simpson said that, "The two prominent advantages of this secret are its simplicity and its universality. It is not a complicated mass of petty rites, ceremonies or enactments but one simple and comprehensive prescription, covering everything, and needing only to be habitually applied; namely, Christ for everything. And as it is so simple, so it is universal in its application. There is no side of human nature to which it does not apply, whether the inner life of the soul, the needs of the body, the circumstances of life, or the exigencies of duty and work."

Watchman Nee, the Chinese Christian leader who was martyred for his faith, said, "This is a matter that God delights to bring to us with a new flash of understanding. Suddenly one day we see that Christ is our life (Colossians 3-4). That day everything is changed. There is a day . . . when we see that Christ within us is our life. That too alters our whole outlook . . . then we begin to know Christ's fullness, and to marvel that we have been so stupid hitherto as to remain poor in God's storehouse."

My Daily Journal

On what date did you read this lesson ? _________
Study to show thyself approved unto God, a workman that needs not to be ashamed (2 Tim 2:15).

What Christ-like deed have you done?

____

____

Why do you call me Lord, Lord and not do the things that I say (Luke 6:46)?

Which temptations have you overcome?

____

Blessed is the man that endures temptation: for when he is tried, he shall receive the crown of life (James 1:12).

Which temptations have you yield to?

____

If we confess our sins, he is faithful and just to forgive us our sins, and to cleanse us from all unrighteousness (I John 1:9).

**CHAPTER
NINE**

THE SECRET OF THE SUBSTITUTE

**When we have failed to find the success,
peace, power, and joy we want in life,
we can exchange our life for a new one,
the life of Jesus Christ.**

Jesus Christ does not want to merely help you; He wants to replace your losing life with His winning life. In a word, He wants to be your substitute.

A game of football gave me my first lesson in what Bible students call "substitution"—what Jesus Christ does for us and in us. The meaning of the word was deeply and dearly impressed upon me in a game against Gloster, Mississippi.

I was playing center at 155 pounds. The opposing guard weighed 255. He was not only too big to block, I couldn't even see around him. By the end of the third quarter we were three touchdowns behind, and I had a busted nose and fractured ribs.

It was too late to win the game; I was just trying to survive. So I snapped the ball, brought my fist up, and tried to run it through his head. He turned for a flip and got up with one eye closed. But on the next play I had to snap the ball for a punt. This means putting your head down between your legs and hoping you live through the play. I saw the ball hit the fullback Hubert Polk's hands.

The next sight I saw was Dr. Dick Munson's face. Through a maze of stars I could barely make him out. He was slapping my face, holding smelling salts under my nose and saying, "Breathe deep, breathe deep." I raised up just long enough to look out on the field and see a wonderful sight—Rupert Thompson. He was my substitute. I grinned and lay back and spent the rest of the game in Dr. Dick Munson's lap. That is the night the word "substitute" became very precious to me.

When I first heard someone say, "Jesus Christ came into the world to be our substitute," I understood exactly what he meant.
On the cross of Calvary He took my place in death. He died a death I could never die. The wages of my sin were eternal death. I could have died a million years and never paid the penalty. But that day at the cross Jesus died a physical and spiritual death for me.

But that is only half the story. Fifty days later, on the day of Pentecost, Jesus came back by His Spirit to be my substitute in life. He came back to live a life I could never have lived. We cannot keep the Ten Commandments. We cannot love our enemies. The only one who can live such a life is Jesus Christ. At Pentecost He came to live that life in us.

My Daily Journal

On what date did you read this lesson ?________

Study to show thyself approved unto God, a workman that needs not to be ashamed (2 Tim 2:15).

What Christ-like deed have you done?

____

____

Why do you call me Lord, Lord and not do the things that I say (Luke 6:46)?

Which temptations have you overcome?

____

____

Blessed is the man that endures temptation: for when he is tried, he shall receive the crown of life (James 1:12).

Which temptations have you yield to?

____

____

If we confess our sins, he is faithful and just to forgive us our sins, and to cleanse us from all unrighteousness (I John 1:9).

CHAPTER
TEN

SOAR HIGHER IN LIFE

**When you discover, as Paul did, that
"Christ lives in me" then
you can also say with Paul,
"I can do all things through Christ
who strengthens me"**

Zig Ziglar, God's ambassador of success, told this story: "Several years ago, a balloon salesman was selling balloons on the streets of New York City. When business got a little slow, he would release a balloon. As it floated into the air, a fresh crowd of buyers would gather and his business would pick up for a few minutes. He alternated the colors, first releasing a white one. Then a red one and later a yellow one. After a time, a little Negro boy tugged on his coat sleeve, looked the balloon salesman in the eye and asked a penetrating question. 'Mister, if you released a black balloon, would it go up?' The balloon salesman . . . said, 'Son, it's what's inside those balloons that make them go up.' Yes, the balloon salesman was 'right.' I'm also 'right' when I tell you, it's what's inside you that will make you go up."[4]

The great secret of the winning life is what is on

the inside. When you discover, as Paul did, that "Christ lives in me" (Galatians 2:20), then you can also say with Paul, "I can do all things through Christ which strengthens me" (Philippians 4:13).

Then you can rise to new heights in life, as the balloon rises above the earth.

My Daily Journal

On what date did you read this lesson ?________

Study to show thyself approved unto God, a workman that needs not to be ashamed (2 Tim 2:15).

What Christ-like deed have you done?

____

____

Why do you call me Lord, Lord and not do the things that I say (Luke 6:46)?

Which temptations have you overcome?

____

____

Blessed is the man that endures temptation: for when he is tried, he shall receive the crown of life (James 1:12).

Which temptations have you yield to?

____

____

If we confess our sins, he is faithful and just to forgive us our sins, and to cleanse us from all unrighteousness (I John 1:9).

CHAPTER
ELEVEN

EXPERIENCE THE EXCITING EXCHANGED LIFE

Jesus Christ did not come to try to change our old nature, to improve our old morality, to soften our old heart. He came that we might exchange our life for His life.

The true Christian life, though it may result in many changes, technically speaking, is not a changed life. It is an exchanged life. There is a vast difference. Jesus Christ did not come to try to change our old nature, to improve our old morality, to soften our old heart. He came that we might exchange our life for His life.

Paul made it so simple with these words: "I am crucified with Christ: nevertheless I live; yet not I, but Christ lives in me: and the life which I now live in the flesh I live by the faith of the Son of God, who loved me, and gave himself for me" (Galatians 2:20). Paul did not try to improve himself. He said, I "have no confidence in the flesh" (Philippians 3:3). He reckoned he was only worthy of execution. So he sentenced himself to death—to the cross. He said, "I am crucified with Christ. I condemned my old life." Yet he lived! And how? He explains, "It is no longer I, but Christ that lives in me." It wasn't the same old "I" polished up, improved, or made over. It was Christ living inside his body.

Exchanging unsatisfactory merchandise is good, exchanging an unsatisfactory life is far better

We are thankful for stores that allow us to exchange merchandise that is not satisfactory. We can return it for something better. We can also thank God that He makes exchanges. When we have failed to find the success, peace, power, and joy we want in life, we can exchange our life for a new one, the life of Jesus Christ. After that we can say with Paul, "It is no longer I but Christ that lives in me."

My Daily Journal

On what date did you read this lesson ?________

Study to show thyself approved unto God, a workman that needs not to be ashamed (2 Tim 2:15).

What Christ-like deed have you done?

____

____

Why do you call me Lord, Lord and not do the things that I say (Luke 6:46)?

Which temptations have you overcome?

____

____

Blessed is the man that endures temptation: for when he is tried, he shall receive the crown of life (James 1:12).

Which temptations have you yield to?

____

____

If we confess our sins, he is faithful and just to forgive us our sins, and to cleanse us from all unrighteousness (I John 1:9).

**CHAPTER
TWELVE**

THE WINNER'S HOME

On the day of Pentecost, God moved into His new home, the bodies of believers

Jesus Christ, the ultimate Winner, can actually make your body His home. This is what He died for. There were many things that happened when Jesus Christ hung between heaven and earth on Golgotha. One of the most significant things was that while He was dying the earth shook and the curtain in the temple rent in twain. That curtain separated the people that came to worship from the holy of holies. Only the high priest was allowed behind the curtain. Once a year he tied a rope around his foot and cautiously entered into the dwelling place of God. The rope was to enable the people to pull him out if he died behind the curtain. It was the only way, since they were excluded.

Jesus moved into the believer's bodies

When Christ died on the cross, there was an earthquake and the temple curtain was split from top to bottom. God moved out of His old house, the temple's holy of holies. Fifty days later, on the day of Pentecost, He moved into His new home, the bodies of believers. The partition between sinful men and a holy God has been removed by the atonement Jesus made.

Since that day God can enter the bodies of all who have been cleansed by the blood of Jesus. You can now have a golden treasure in your earthen vessel.

My Daily Journal

On what date did you read this lesson ? _________

Study to show thyself approved unto God, a workman that needs not to be ashamed (2 Tim 2:15).

What Christ-like deed have you done?

____

____

Why do you call me Lord, Lord and not do the things that I say (Luke 6:46)?

Which temptations have you overcome?

____

____

Blessed is the man that endures temptation: for when he is tried, he shall receive the crown of life (James 1:12).

Which temptations have you yield to?

____

____

If we confess our sins, he is faithful and just to forgive us our sins, and to cleanse us from all unrighteousness (I John 1:9).

CHAPTER
THIRTEEN

TRIUMPH THROUGH A POWERFUL PURPOSE

God disappeared from sight in Jesus' body that He might appear again throughout the world in the bodies of thousands of true believers

From the dawn of redemption God's purpose was to come live inside you. He first created man in His own image. He made him capable of love and fellowship with Himself. He placed him in a paradise, the Garden of Eden. And God occupied His time walking with man in that garden. But then the wicked mistrust and rebellion of man, called sin, severed the relationship. A holy God could not compromise His fellowship with unholy man. Man and God were separated.

But God does not give up. Jesus went to the cross and died for sin. Through His atonement, unholy man can be made clean. The fellowship that was broken in Eden is restored at Calvary. God and man are reunited. Christ comes to live in our hearts. This is the mystery of the entire universe. And this is the purpose of man, to know God and to be united with God.

Jesus Christ came to earth to bring man a wonderful new dimension of living. He said, "I am come that you might have life, and that you might have it more abundantly" (John 10:10).

The mystery of a winning life

This new abundant dimension comes through having Jesus Christ live inside you. Jesus said in John 14:15, "And I will pray the Father, and he shall give you another Comforter . . . whom the world cannot receive, because it sees him not neither knows him: but you know him; for he dwells with you, and shall be in you. I will not leave you comfortless: I will come to you . . . . At that day you shall know that I am in my Father, and you in me, and I in you . . . . If a man love me, he will keep my words: and my Father will love him, and we will come unto him, and make our abode with him" (John 14:16-18, 20, 23).

Jesus said He would not leave us, He would come to us, and He would be in us. This is the amazing mystery of the life of Jesus Christ. It did not end at a grave and it was not contained within one body. By His spirit He has come to live in all that will receive Him.

Before the day of Pentecost one body had contained Jesus Christ. After the day of Pentecost all bodies can contain Jesus Christ. God disappeared from sight in Jesus' body that He might appear again throughout the world in the bodies of thousands of true believers.

In the last book of the Bible, Jesus Christ wrote letters to the seven churches in Asia. When He wrote the last letter to the last church, He closed it with a promise of living inside our bodies. Jesus said, "Behold, I stand at the door, and knock: if any man hear my voice, and open the door, I will come in to him, and will sup with him, and he with me" (Revelations 3:20). Jesus wanted to make it so clear no one could possibly miss it. He said we are like a house: someone knocks; you open the door. They come in. And that's the way it is with life. Jesus knocks on the door of our heart. We open. And God comes in to live within us.

My Daily Journal

On what date did you read this lesson ?___________

Study to show thyself approved unto God, a workman that needs not to be ashamed (2 Tim 2:15).

What Christ-like deed have you done?

____

____

Why do you call me Lord, Lord and not do the things that I say (Luke 6:46)?

Which temptations have you overcome?

____

____

Blessed is the man that endures temptation: for when he is tried, he shall receive the crown of life (James 1:12).

Which temptations have you yield to?

____

____

If we confess our sins, he is faithful and just to forgive us our sins, and to cleanse us from all unrighteousness (I John 1:9).

CHAPTER
FOURTEEN

KNOWING HEAVEN
IS ON YOUR SIDE

**To please God we must simply allow Jesus
to live in us and reveal Himself to others.
It is that simple. Just reveal Christ through
the life you live and the words you speak.**

Perhaps the most frustrating religious question of all ages has been: "How can a mortal man please God?" Paul plainly answered, "It pleased God, who separated me from my mother's womb, and called me by His grace, to reveal His Son in me" (Galatians 1: 15, 16).

To please God we must simply allow Jesus to live in us and reveal Himself to others. It is that simple. Just reveal Christ through the life you live and the words you speak.

Be sure that nothing else will suffice. Doing great works, building massive buildings, giving huge amounts of money, preaching and teaching, or even being a missionary will not be of any pleasure to God unless through it all you are revealing Christ.

My Daily Journal

On what date did you read this lesson ?_________

Study to show thyself approved unto God, a workman that needs not to be ashamed (2 Tim 2:15).

What Christ-like deed have you done?

____

____

Why do you call me Lord, Lord and not do the things that I say (Luke 6:46)?

Which temptations have you overcome?

____

____

Blessed is the man that endures temptation: for when he is tried, he shall receive the crown of life (James 1:12).

Which temptations have you yield to?

____

____

If we confess our sins, he is faithful and just to forgive us our sins, and to cleanse us from all unrighteousness (I John 1:9).

CHAPTER
FIFTEEN

EXPERIENCE THE MOST MYSTERIOUS MIRACLE

**The miracle of the virgin birth was the
Holy Spirit formed Christ in Mary.
Today that miracle is being repeated
thousands of times in every believer.**

A man told me once, "Moody, I just can't accept the Bible. There are so many things in it that seem preposterous. Now you take the virgin birth of Jesus Christ. Do you actually expect me to believe that a virgin girl had a baby?" I replied, "That is just a very, very small miracle. If you find it startling to believe that God formed Jesus in the womb of the virgin girl Mary, that is a small thing compared to this—God has, also, formed Jesus in the heart of every believer! The miracle of the virgin birth was the Holy Spirit formed Christ in Mary. Today that miracle is being repeated thousands of times as the same Holy Spirit forms Jesus Christ inside all who receive Him." That is the most amazing, the most exciting, the most fantastic miracle with which I am acquainted. That God has formed His Son in the unworthy heart of this poor frail sinner, Moody Adams, and has repeated it in millions of other lives. Praise God!

My Daily Journal

On what date did you read this lesson ?_________

Study to show thyself approved unto God, a workman that needs not to be ashamed (2 Tim 2:15).

What Christ-like deed have you done?

____

____

Why do you call me Lord, Lord and not do the things that I say (Luke 6:46)?

Which temptations have you overcome?

____

____

Blessed is the man that endures temptation: for when he is tried, he shall receive the crown of life (James 1:12).

Which temptations have you yield to?

____

____

If we confess our sins, he is faithful and just to forgive us our sins, and to cleanse us from all unrighteousness (I John 1:9).

CHAPTER
SIXTEEN

ESCAPE THE
LOSER'S SNARE

**The error of the Corinthians was rooted in
not knowing that God lived inside their bodies.**

The basic problems of the human race could be
solved if they only knew where God was. The world
thinks Jesus Christ is still in the grave; it therefore
has no hope. Many religious people think God lives in
their sanctuary, "the house of God", they have no
power. Only a few have discovered He is living inside
their bodies! They have both hope and power.

All the problems of the Christian church were
previewed in the church at Corinth. They were
analyzed in Paul's letter to that church. The
Corinthians were carnal, worldly, divided, immoral
people calling themselves Christians. Paul not only
discussed the fruits of the problem, but he put his
finger on the taproot of the problem. I Corinthians
3:16, 17 says, "Know you not that you are the temple
of God, and that the Spirit of God dwells in you? If
any man defile the temple of God, him shall God
destroy; for the temple of God is holy, which temple

you are." Again Paul exclaims, "What? Know you not that your body is the temple of the Holy Ghost which is in you, which you have of God, and you are not your own? For you are bought with a price: therefore glorify God in your body, and in your spirit, which are God's" (I Corinthians 6:19, 20).

The error of the Corinthians was rooted in not knowing that God lived inside their bodies. This same error is propagated today in vast areas of religion. The minister refers to his church's main building as a sanctuary. The people have been thoroughly indoctrinated in this error that the church house is God's house. Listen to the mother say, "Son, now you behave, we are going into God's house." When we discover that our body is God's house, we want to behave all the time.

The finance committee appeals, "Now we are going to have to sacrifice, but remember that we are out to build the house of God." The result has been that we have succeeded in raising far more money than any generation of Christians has ever raised for buildings. At the same time we have also succeeded in living the most immoral lives any generation of "Christians" has ever lived. Seventy percent of all inmates in one Southern penitentiary were found to be active church members!

The problem is seen again in prayer meetings where people pray, "Lord, send your Spirit." If the apostle Paul were to attend one of these prayer meetings, he would probably walk over and tap the brother on the shoulder and say, "What, know you not that your body is the temple of the Holy Ghost which is in you" (I Corinthians 6:19).

Dr. A. B. Simpson points out two thrilling facts about this marvelous mystery of Christ living in us. "It is not a complicated mass of petty rites, ceremonies or enactments but one simple and comprehensive prescription, covering everything and needing only to be habitually applied; namely Christ for everything and as it is so simple so it is universal in its application there is no side of human nature to which it does not apply, whether the inner life of the soul, the needs of the body, the circumstances of life, or the exigencies of duty and work."

My Daily Journal

On what date did you read this lesson ?_________

Study to show thyself approved unto God, a workman that needs not to be ashamed (2 Tim 2:15).

What Christ-like deed have you done?

____

____

Why do you call me Lord, Lord and not do the things that I say (Luke 6:46)?

Which temptations have you overcome?

____

Blessed is the man that endures temptation: for when he is tried, he shall receive the crown of life (James 1:12).

Which temptations have you yield to?

____

If we confess our sins, he is faithful and just to forgive us our sins, and to cleanse us from all unrighteousness (I John 1:9).

**CHAPTER
SEVENTEEN**

TURN YOUR DEFEATS INTO VICTORIES

**Any ordinary person can become a success
just as Gideon did, by becoming
merely clothes for God to wear around.**

The great explanation of the victorious life is found in the life of Gideon. The Bible explains the fantastic success of this man who won victories against impossible odds. Scripture said the Spirit of the Lord "clothed himself with Gideon" (Judges 6:34). That was all Gideon was, just clothes for the Holy Spirit to wear around. He was just the container; inside was the Creator. God was in him doing the planning, making the decisions, encouraging, and giving the victory. Any ordinary person can become a success just as Gideon did, by becoming merely clothes for God to wear around.

The key to making every day
a winning day

No longer do we have to get up in the morning

saying, "God, I'll do my best today to go out and live right, to treat people right and work for you today." Now we can get up and say with a salute, "Lord, here I am reporting for duty, You know I am very weak and foolish. Though I am frail you are in me, and you have all power. Here is my mouth, if you want to talk to anyone today, you can use it. Here are my feet, if you want to go anywhere today, you can use them. Here are my hands, whatever work you choose to do, they are available. I exchange my life for Your Life."

A man cannot determine his true wealth by looking at his financial statement; he must look at his heart. You may be very poor and frail, but it doesn't matter when Christ is "in you." You have golden treasures in your earthen vessel!

My Daily Journal

On what date did you read this lesson ?________

Study to show thyself approved unto God, a workman that needs not to be ashamed (2 Tim 2:15).

What Christ-like deed have you done?

____

____

Why do you call me Lord, Lord and not do the things that I say (Luke 6:46)?

Which temptations have you overcome?

____

____

Blessed is the man that endures temptation: for when he is tried, he shall receive the crown of life (James 1:12).

Which temptations have you yield to?

____

____

If we confess our sins, he is faithful and just to forgive us our sins, and to cleanse us from all unrighteousness (I John 1:9).

CHAPTER
EIGHTEEN

SEIZE THIS FANTASTIC STUDY IN SUCCESS

You have the potential
of doing what God can do!

The key to success is found in a glove. Look at one. It is flimsy and powerless. It cannot move. It cannot do anything. But pick it up and put your hand in it and at that moment the glove becomes capable of doing anything your hand can do.

Notice this. It doesn't matter about the age of the glove or whether it is tattered or well cared for. It doesn't matter what color the glove is, nor whether it is costly or cheap. The moment the hand goes in the glove, the glove instantly becomes capable of doing anything the hand can do.

Likewise, you may be very weak . . . but the moment you receive Jesus Christ into your weak body, you have the potential of doing what God can do!

John 1:12 says, "But as many as received him, to them gave he power to become the sons of God." That is the key to power. The moment you receive Him, you receive the power of God. Galatians 2:8 says that Jesus Christ was "effectual" in Peter and "mighty" in Paul.

Paul prayed for all men to gain the riches of this power, "That he would grant you, according to the riches of his glory, to be strengthened with might by his Spirit in the inner man; That Christ may dwell in your hearts by faith" (Ephesians 3:16, 17).

My Daily Journal

On what date did you read this lesson ?________
Study to show thyself approved unto God, a workman that needs not to be ashamed (2 Tim 2:15).

What Christ-like deed have you done?
____

____

Why do you call me Lord, Lord and not do the things that I say (Luke 6:46)?

Which temptations have you overcome?
____

____

Blessed is the man that endures temptation: for when he is tried, he shall receive the crown of life (James 1:12).

Which temptations have you yield to?
____

____

If we confess our sins, he is faithful and just to forgive us our sins, and to cleanse us from all unrighteousness (I John 1:9).

**CHAPTER
NINETEEN**

MASTER THE REWARDING RIDDLE OF RECEPTIVITY

**"Man's chief function is receptivity,
or receiving from God,
not Activity, or doing for God."
—*Norman Grubb***

Man's chief function is Receptivity, or receiving from God, not Activity, or doing for God. —*Norman Grubb*

My head whirled with the wonder of it all. I cried. I laughed. I thanked God all the way to work the following morning. It just seemed too wonderful—too wonderful and far too simple.

In one night of my life I had learned a simple fact that was revolutionizing my whole life.

Before that night, I had thought that everything in life had to be earned, fought for, and won. "Nobody gets anything for nothing." Even God helped only those "who help themselves," therefore, to me Christianity consisted of me doing things for God:

going to church, staying sober, telling the truth, etc. For two years I had struggled through such "activity," trying to make a Christian out of myself. It is easy for a person to say, "Anyone can live a Christian life if they just try." It is easy to say, if that person has not tried. But I had tried. I found it not only difficult, but impossible. But one night a man in Jackson, Mississippi explained this passage in John 1:12 to me: "As many as received him to them gave he power to become the sons of God."

That verse opened the door to a New World. All I had to do was "receive" him. He gave the "power." Norman Grubb stated it this way, "Man's chief function is RECEPTIVITY, or receiving from God, not ACTIVITY, or doing for God."

Man's chief function is to receive from God

As I read the Bible, I discovered RECEPTIVITY was a thread running through all of Scripture. It traced the key to all of heaven's gifts:

"We also joy in God through our Lord Jesus Christ, by whom we have now RECEIVED the atonement" (Romans 5:11).

"Shall RECEIVE remission of sins" (Acts 10:43).

"That they may RECEIVE forgiveness" (Acts 26:18).

"We have RECEIVED mercy" (II Corinthians 4:1).

"Which have RECEIVED the Holy Ghost" (Acts 10:47).

"You shall RECEIVE power" (Acts 1:8).

"Man hath RECEIVED the gift" (I Peter 4: 10).

"RECEIVING the end of your faith, even the salvation of your souls" (I Peter 1:9).

"Asks and you shall RECEIVE, that your joy may be full" (John 16:24).

"You shall RECEIVE a crown of glory" (I Peter 5:4).

My Daily Journal

On what date did you read this lesson ?________
Study to show thyself approved unto God, a workman that needs not to be ashamed (2 Tim 2:15).

What Christ-like deed have you done?

____

____

Why do you call me Lord, Lord and not do the things that I say (Luke 6:46)?

Which temptations have you overcome?

____

____

Blessed is the man that endures temptation: for when he is tried, he shall receive the crown of life (James 1:12).

Which temptations have you yield to?

____

____

If we confess our sins, he is faithful and just to forgive us our sins, and to cleanse us from all unrighteousness (I John 1:9).

**CHAPTER
TWENTY**

THE KEY TO
THE MYSTERIES
OF OUR UNIVERSE

**Apart from receiving God's "life breath,"
we would have never been anything
more than a mound of dirt.**

Jesus said, "A man can receive nothing, except it be given him from heaven" (John 3:27). "Nothing" covers not only spiritual gifts but also every speck of dirt in the entire universe. It all comes through RECEPTIVITY.

Where did this planet come from? Did you create it? I didn't. "Who else but God goes back and forth to heaven? Who else holds the wind in His fists, and wraps up the oceans in His cloak? Who but God has created the world? If there is any other, what is his name, and his son's name if you can tell" (Proverbs 30:4).

The earth we stand on, the sunshine that warms us, the rain that brings our water, the food we eat, and the air we breathe are all made by God and given to us by God. We have only received them. Nature has a thousand voices teaching us RECEPTIVITY.

This question is a stunning one to proud, godless men, but reason demands it is answered. "What have you that you did not receive? Now if you did not receive it, why do you glory as if you had not received it?" (I Corinthians 4:7). God gives life. We received it. "God breathed into man and he became a living soul" (Genesis 2:7). Apart from receiving God's "life breath," we would have never been anything more than a mound of dirt.

All of the sufferings of life are teaching us receptivity

The reason Satan was allowed to tempt man in the Garden of Eden was not to test man, but to teach man his need for God. God knew man would fall. This was why, before He even created us, much less tested us, He prepared to redeem us "with the precious blood of Christ, as of a lamb without blemish and without spot: Who verily was foreordained before the foundation of the world" (I Peter 1:19, 20).

Cursed by his fall, man learns through his tears, toil, pain, and death that he needs God. The tuition is high, very high. But all the sufferings of life are worth it if they teach us we are not "self-sufficient."

Every pain is a messenger crying, "You need God's comfort, God's strength, God's guidance and God's peace." All suffering tells us of our need to "receive" from God. All trials "crowd us to Christ."

My Daily Journal

On what date did you read this lesson ?_________

Study to show thyself approved unto God, a workman that needs not to be ashamed (2 Tim 2:15).

What Christ-like deed have you done?

____

____

Why do you call me Lord, Lord and not do the things that I say (Luke 6:46)?

Which temptations have you overcome?

____

____

Blessed is the man that endures temptation: for when he is tried, he shall receive the crown of life (James 1:12).

Which temptations have you yield to?

____

____

If we confess our sins, he is faithful and just to forgive us our sins, and to cleanse us from all unrighteousness (I John 1:9).

CHAPTER
TWENTY-ONE

GOD GIVES, WE SIMPLY RECEIVE

We were made to be merely the receivers, with God the giver.

The basic foundation of the good news of the Gospel is "God so loved the world that He gave" (John 3:16). That is the key. God gives. Man receives.

Jesus said, "Freely you have received" (Matthew 10:8). How do men obtain salvation? They received it as a free gift.

The Bible says, "Believing, you rejoice with joy unspeakable and full of glory: Receiving the end of your faith, even the salvation of your souls" (I Peter 1:8, 9).

The exciting fact many have not understood is that God not only wants to give you salvation but also "shall supply all of your needs, according to his riches" (Philippians 4:19).

God's plan is for us to live every day of the Christian life just exactly as we began it. Colossians 2:6 says, "As you have therefore received Christ Jesus the Lord, so walk you in him." No instructions could be clearer. We received Christ as completely helpless sinners and so obtain salvation. Even so, we live as completely helpless saints, receiving everything from Jesus.

The Holy Spirit comes through receptivity

The Holy Spirit is imparted to men through RECEPTIVITY. "He (Jesus) breathed on them and says unto them, RECEIVE you the Holy Ghost" (John 20:22). "Then Peter said unto them, 'Repent, and be baptized every one of you in the name of Jesus Christ . . . and you shall RECEIVE the gift of the Holy Ghost'" (Acts 2:38). Not by working, neither by begging nor bargaining, but the Holy Spirit comes when we merely receive Him!

And this is what we were made for, to receive the life of God. We were not made to live holy by our own efforts, but to be containers for the Holy One. We were made to be merely the containers, with God the contents. We were made to be merely the receivers, with God the giver.

Everything man gets from God comes by the grace of a giving God to receiving men. Nothing is merited by our activity. He supplies all our needs through his "riches in grace." That does not mean that God does some of it, or most of it. It means God does it all. "And if by grace, then it is no more of works: otherwise grace is no more grace" (Romans 11:6).

George Trumbull said, "Many Christians . . . mistakenly think as I did, that they must have some part in overcoming the power of their sin; that their efforts, their will, their determination, strengthened and helped by the power of Christ, is the way to victory. And as long as they mistakenly believe this they are as doomed to defeat as they would be doomed to eternal death if their salvation depended upon their working with Christ to pay the penalty of their sin."

My Daily Journal

On what date did you read this lesson ?________
Study to show thyself approved unto God, a workman that needs not to be ashamed (2 Tim 2:15).

What Christ-like deed have you done?

____

____

Why do you call me Lord, Lord and not do the things that I say (Luke 6:46)?

Which temptations have you overcome?

____

Blessed is the man that endures temptation: for when he is tried, he shall receive the crown of life (James 1:12).

Which temptations have you yield to?

____

If we confess our sins, he is faithful and just to forgive us our sins, and to cleanse us from all unrighteousness (I John 1:9).

**CHAPTER
TWENTY-TWO**

THE KEY TO THE LIFE
OF JESUS CHRIST

**"According as his divine power
hath given unto us all things
that pertain unto life and godliness"
—II Peter 1:3**

Jesus was the great example of receptivity. He constantly went about saying He was nothing. All He had, He received from His Father. "The Son can do nothing of himself" (John 5:19); "I do nothing of myself" (John 8:28); "My doctrine is not mine, but his that sent me" (John 7:16); "The words that I speak unto you I speak not of myself: but the Father that dwells in me, He does the works" (John 14:10); "For He received from God the Father honor and glory" (II Peter 1:17), And to us the Lord Jesus Christ said, "I have given you an example" (John 13:15). The example is this. God gives the life, the words and the power. We only receive. Jesus said, "Abide in me, and I in you . . . for without me you can do Nothing" (John 15:5).

Receptivity and the rapture

Suppose a group of Christians started meeting three times a week to practice high jumping so they could "leap" up into the air to meet Jesus when He returns. We would laugh at such a ridiculous exercise. Of course, we are to be caught up by Jesus' power, not propelled by our own leaping.

I Thessalonians 4:16, 17 says, "For the Lord himself shall descend from heaven with a shout, with the voice of the archangel, and with the trump of God: and the dead in Christ shall rise first: Then we which are alive and remain shall be caught up together with them in the clouds, to meet the Lord in the air: and so shall we ever be with the Lord." Christians shall be CAUGHT up when Christ returns. The verb is passive. We shall not LEAP up but "We shall be CAUGHT up."

We can see how funny it is to think a man could ascend up into heaven by his own activity. But it is difficult to see it is just as absurd to think a man can live the Christian life by his own activity.

At the rapture we will be caught up by "His power." Today we are kept by "His power" (I Peter 1:5).

Likewise, we witness by His power: "You shall receive power, after that the Holy Ghost is come upon you: and you shall be witnesses" (Acts 1:8).

We are made strong by His power: "strengthened with all might, according to his glorious power" (Colossians 1:11).

We overcome Satan by His power: "Behold I give you power . . . over all the power of the enemy" (Luke 10:19).

We receive all things by His power: "According as

his divine power hath given unto us all things that pertain unto life and godliness" (II Peter 1:3).

In every phase of the Christian life it is just as true as in the rapture. God does it all. He bestows the blessing; we are the benefactors.

My Daily Journal

On what date did you read this lesson ?________
Study to show thyself approved unto God, a workman that needs not to be ashamed (2 Tim 2:15).

What Christ-like deed have you done?
____
____

Why do you call me Lord, Lord and not do the things that I say (Luke 6:46)?

Which temptations have you overcome?
____
____

Blessed is the man that endures temptation: for when he is tried, he shall receive the crown of life (James 1:12).

Which temptations have you yield to?
____
____

If we confess our sins, he is faithful and just to forgive us our sins, and to cleanse us from all unrighteousness (I John 1:9).

CHAPTER
TWENTY-THREE

CHRIST MOTIVATES US FROM WITHIN

**A furnace can't produce anything
by its own "activity." But when it "receives"
the fuel and the fire, then it becomes
a dynamo of power.**

The question naturally rises: "If people believe that, will they try to live right or work for God?" The answer lies in another question: "What is the best way to motivate people to live right and work hard?" Is it through fear, duty, tradition? Or is it through love?

The hardest working, most dedicated Christian that ever lived was undoubtedly Paul. He said, "The love of Christ constrains us" (II Corinthians 5:14). Paul was motivated by God's love. Henry Drummon called love "the greatest thing in the world."

Now if love is the greatest motivating force, then it follows that those who have the greatest awareness of God's love will work the hardest and live the cleanest. And who has a greater awareness of God's love than those who are daily receiving everything from God?

The great genuine dedicated Christians are not

products of legalist nagging to "live better, do better, or work harder." They are the result of the discovery that God loves them and wants to do everything for them and through them.

The hard working apostle Paul said, "Whereunto I also labor, striving according to His work, which works in me mightily" (Colossians 1:29). That was the key to the hardest working Christian life ever lived. He received his energy, his driving force, from the God who had come to live in him. You can do the same.

A furnace can't produce anything by its own "activity." But when it "receives" the fuel and the fire, then it becomes a dynamo of power. Likewise, when a man receives the fire of the Holy Ghost within his heart, he moves. A dynamo of energy explodes within him.

Jeremiah once wanted to stop serving God. He said he would quit, but he couldn't. There was fire in his bones. "Then I said, 'I will not make mention of him, nor speak any more in his name.' But his word was in mine heart as a burning fire shut up in my bones, and was weary with forbearing, and I could not stay" (Jeremiah 20:9). The explosive force within Jeremiah made it impossible for him to quit.

My Daily Journal

On what date did you read this lesson ?________

Study to show thyself approved unto God, a workman that needs not to be ashamed (2 Tim 2:15).

What Christ-like deed have you done?

____

____

Why do you call me Lord, Lord and not do the things that I say (Luke 6:46)?

Which temptations have you overcome?

____

____

Blessed is the man that endures temptation: for when he is tried, he shall receive the crown of life (James 1:12).

Which temptations have you yield to?

____

____

If we confess our sins, he is faithful and just to forgive us our sins, and to cleanse us from all unrighteousness (I John 1:9).

CHAPTER
TWENTY-FOUR

EVERYTHING GOOD IS RECEIVED FROM GOD

Look at the prodigal standing there . . . receiving a
welcome . . . receiving a kiss . . . receiving a
ring . . . receiving a robe . . . receiving a feast.
Receptivity overwhelms our little hearts,
but it is true. The Father wants to provide
for you and me, despite our unworthiness
and our wanderings. He loves us!

All good activity has to be done by God for "all our
righteousnesses are as filthy rags" (Isaiah 64:6).
Scripture says, "They that are in the flesh cannot
please God. But you are not in the flesh, but in the
Spirit, if so be that the Spirit of God dwell in
you" (Romans 8:8, 9). But man can receive the Holy
Spirit. Then the Holy Spirit can act through that man
in a way that will please God.

All good activity has to be done by God or God
would not get all the glory. Paul said, "But we have
this treasure in earthen vessels, that the excellency of

the power may be of God, and not of us" (II Corinthians 4:7). God shares everything else with us except His glory. Man's function is simply to be a cheap, worthless, "earthen vessel." This way the "excellency of the power" is of God and God gets all the glory.

This question came to the *Sunday School Times* office: "What do you consider the most dangerous heresy of today?" Mr. Trumbull answered as follows, "The most dangerous (heresy) is the emphasis that is given, right in the professing Christian church itself, on what we do for God instead of what God does for us."

Perhaps you have struggled for years trying to live for God and work for God. But now you see that God wants you to be merely the receiver of His blessing, the tool for His work, and the container for His life. Receptivity means the struggle is over and the frustration is gone!

Jesus' story of the prodigal son makes RECEPTIVITY very clear. A father gives his son his portion of his inheritance. The son receives it. But as soon as he has received the money, RECEPTIVITY stops. He does not wish to receive instruction, correction, wisdom, guidance nor discipline—only money. With the money, he is ready to launch his own "activities." He leaves home. He leaves his father. All his hopes for happiness center in his activities with wine and women.

Poor young man. He hasn't discovered the mysterious key to life. As always, his "activities" fail to provide happiness. Why, his father's servants are better off than he is! They are receiving their protection and provisions from the father. Broken and disillusioned, he heads back home.

Now what does the father say? "Do penance," "Work as a slave" or "Merit my home"? No! No! The father takes up where he left off when his son went away . . . giving. He gives a running welcome . . . he gives a kiss . . . he gives a ring . . . he gives a robe . . . he gives a feast.

Jesus' story unveils life's great key—RECEPTIVITY. Look at the prodigal standing there . . . receiving a welcome . . . receiving a kiss . . . receiving a ring . . . receiving a robe . . . receiving a feast.

RECEPTIVITY overwhelms our little hearts, but it is true. The Father wants to provide for you and me, despite our unworthiness and our wanderings. He loves us!

My Daily Journal

On what date did you read this lesson ?_________

Study to show thyself approved unto God, a workman that needs not to be ashamed (2 Tim 2:15).

What Christ-like deed have you done?

____

____

Why do you call me Lord, Lord and not do the things that I say (Luke 6:46)?

Which temptations have you overcome?

____

____

Blessed is the man that endures temptation: for when he is tried, he shall receive the crown of life (James 1:12).

Which temptations have you yield to?

____

____

If we confess our sins, he is faithful and just to forgive us our sins, and to cleanse us from all unrighteousness (I John 1:9).

CHAPTER
TWENTY-FIVE

______

START OVER WITH A NEW SELF-IMAGE

Daily the vessel of clay is made to know its weakness, so that daily the life of Jesus, which conquers death, might show forth its power.

One of the fantastic riches Christ brings us is a new "self-image." Dr. Maxwell Maltz said that the "self-image," the picture we all have of ourselves, is the key to human personality and human behavior. "Change the self-image and you change the personality and the behavior," said Maltz.

In his book, *Psycho-cybernetics,* Dr. Maltz tells about his discovery of the importance of that little photograph we carry around of ourselves. As a plastic surgeon he could make a woman whose face had been scarred beautiful again. But he discovered that some of the women remained introverted and avoided crowds. Dr. Maltz had removed the ugly scars from their faces, but they still carried around a little mental photograph of themselves with a hideous scar on it.

The scars on their self-image made life unbearable.

Tear up your picture
and take a new one

Dr. Maltz's book shows how we are victimized by our self-image. Millions of people are spending their days in abject misery because they see themselves as losers. Their photograph is a picture of a failure. They see themselves as totally incapable of coping with their circumstances.

The apostle Paul's entire life was changed when his "self-image" changed. It happened the moment he discovered "It is no longer I, but Christ that lives in me" (Galatians 2:20). Paul had once carried around the photograph of a hostile, aggressive, guilt-ridden, wretch of a man. One day he made the great discovery: Jesus Christ was living inside his body. He tore up the old photograph and started carrying a new snapshot of himself. His body was the container for the Creator. Jesus Christ was living inside of him. His whole personality and conduct were revolutionized. As Dr. Maltz said, "Change the self-image and you change the personality and the behavior."

My Daily Journal

On what date did you read this lesson ?________
Study to show thyself approved unto God, a workman that needs not to be ashamed (2 Tim 2:15).

What Christ-like deed have you done?

____

____

Why do you call me Lord, Lord and not do the things that I say (Luke 6:46)?

Which temptations have you overcome?

____

____

Blessed is the man that endures temptation: for when he is tried, he shall receive the crown of life (James 1:12).

Which temptations have you yield to?

____

____

If we confess our sins, he is faithful and just to forgive us our sins, and to cleanse us from all unrighteousness (I John 1:9).

CHAPTER
TWENTY-SIX

THE BENEFITS OF
A DECAYING BODY

*"Daily the vessel of clay is made
to know its weakness, so that daily
the life of Jesus, which conquers death,
might show forth its power."
—Jessie Penn-Lewis*

II Corinthians 4:7 says, "But we have this treasure in earthen vessels, that the excellency of the power may be of God, and not of us." The apostle Paul declared that this treasure is lodged in a body of fragile clay, that so the power (which accomplishes the work) should be God's, and not his own.

Here is how the Bible describes our physical body, the container for the Creator: "A body of fragile clay" (II Corinthians 4:7). "The earthly house of our bodily frame" (II Corinthians 5:1). "This corruptible . . . this mortal" (I Corinthians 15:54). "The body of our humiliation" (Philippians 3:21).

Jessie Penn-Lewis, who wrote during the early 1900s Welsh revival, said, "These words describe the earthen vessel as it always will be until the Lord's appearing. It is 'fragile clay,' and therefore liable to be broken and cannot be used.

"It is called 'the body of our humiliation!' We are children of God, 'heirs of God, and joint-heirs with Christ'; yet we groan, 'longing for the adoption (redemption) which shall ransom our body from its bondage' (Romans 8:23). 'We groan, longing to be clothed upon with our habitation which is from heaven' (II Corinthians 5:2), for it is humiliating to be fettered by a body of clay, subject to the limitation of its laws, whilst in truth a citizen of heaven.

"Daily the vessel of clay is made to know its weakness, so that daily the life of Jesus, which conquers death, might show forth its power. A trembling vessel energized by the Holy Spirit, is the picture before us in the life of Paul. 'I Paul . . . in outward appearance, am base among you' (I who am mean . . . and lowly in outward presence' (II Corinthians 10:1). 'Say they. . . his bodily presence is weak, and his speech contemptible' (II Corinthians 10:10)," says Lewis.

Man thinks so much of outward appearance; of a noble presence; of fluency of speech; of strength of body; but God chooses to do His mightiest work with instruments that are often manifestly weak, base and despised. Moreover He allows them also to remain 'contemptible' in the eyes of others, lest they glory in the instrument, and fail to see the power of God. He was willing to remain in the eyes of others a 'contemptible vessel,' and to accept the truth that in outward appearance, he was "base" in their midst. (See 2 Corinthians 12: 5, 6)."

Do not ever despair

There are two reasons you should not be disgusted over your life, or your looks. First of all, we are all made from "dirt." The Bible declares it and science upholds it; they have never found one ingredient in man that cannot be found in dirt. I really think we look pretty good when you consider what we are made of!

Second, these earthen bodies were designed to contain treasures of gold. The Bible declares, "But we have this treasure in earthen vessels" (II Corinthians 4:7). Jesus Christ has come to live inside our bodies to bring golden treasures to earthen vessels. And nobody should get upset over the poor container when it possesses such contents.

If Jesus Christ lives in you, never think of yourself as inferior to any man or too weak for any situation. If you have received Him, the God of the universe dwells in that body of yours. It is no longer you, but Christ living in you!

My Daily Journal

On what date did you read this lesson ?______

Study to show thyself approved unto God, a workman that needs not to be ashamed (2 Tim 2:15).

What Christ-like deed have you done?

____

____

Why do you call me Lord, Lord and not do the things that I say (Luke 6:46)?

Which temptations have you overcome?

____

____

Blessed is the man that endures temptation: for when he is tried, he shall receive the crown of life (James 1:12).

Which temptations have you yield to?

____

____

If we confess our sins, he is faithful and just to forgive us our sins, and to cleanse us from all unrighteousness (I John 1:9).

**CHAPTER
TWENTY-SEVEN**

GET RID OF GUILT FOREVER

**There are two times in a person's life
when they can be a virgin. One is at birth.
The other is when they come to Jesus' cross!**

There are three mysterious secrets of joy that Jesus Christ brings to the heart of man. The first of these is the joy of forgiveness. People say, "There's no use in crying over spilled milk", and "you can't do anything about the past" or "what's done is done." But the past can be changed. That's what the cross is all about. Jesus died so that every sin we have ever committed can be cleansed.

The moment Christ comes into your heart, all guilt has to go. I Corinthians 6:11 declares, "You are washed, you are sanctified (made clean), you are justified in the name of the Lord Jesus, and by the Spirit of our God." Colossians 2:13 says, "having forgiven you all trespasses." Isaiah 1:18 pleads, "Come now, and let us reason together, says the Lord:

though your sins be as scarlet, they shall be as white as snow; though they be red like crimson, they shall be as wool." Isaiah 6:7 says, "Your iniquity is taken away, and thy sin purged." I John 1:7 says, "The blood of Jesus Christ his Son cleanses us from all sin." (It is good to be forgiven, but it is better to be cleansed.)

On the authority of God's word we can know that the moment we receive Jesus Christ, every sin we have ever committed is cleansed by His blood.

God cannot remember our sins!

If you want to really have an experience in joy, then just sit down and think of every indecent, dirty, ungodly, disappointing thing you have done in your life and then read Hebrews 8:12 and 10:17, "For I will be merciful to their unrighteousness, and their sins and their iniquities will I remember no more." "And their sins and iniquities will I remember no more." That means if you went up to heaven today and said, "God, do you remember the times Moody Adams stole, lied, got drunk, etc.?" God would thoughtfully reply, "Why, if Moody Adams ever did those things, I surely don't remember it." Friend, that's something to shout about. Christ has taken away all the sins of our past. Hallelujah !

Richard Sibbs, an English Puritan, said, "We can do nothing well without joy and a good conscience which is the ground of joy." There it is. The basis of joy. A good conscience. And with Christ in our heart we have not only a good conscience, but also a perfect conscience. Jesus Christ cleanses it from all sin.

The prostitute who became a virgin

Augustine, the early church father, called Mary Magdalene by the most beautiful name I have ever heard a woman called. He addressed the reputed prostitute as the "arch virgin." He is right. There are two times in a person's life when they can be a virgin. One is at birth. The other is when they come to Jesus' cross!

My Daily Journal

On what date did you read this lesson ?________
Study to show thyself approved unto God, a workman that needs not to be ashamed (2 Tim 2:15).

What Christ-like deed have you done?
____

____
Why do you call me Lord, Lord and not do the things that I say (Luke 6:46)?

Which temptations have you overcome?
____

____
Blessed is the man that endures temptation: for when he is tried, he shall receive the crown of life (James 1:12).

Which temptations have you yield to?
____

____
If we confess our sins, he is faithful and just to forgive us our sins, and to cleanse us from all unrighteousness (I John 1:9).

CHAPTER
TWENTY-EIGHT

WIN THE
REWARD OF WISDOM

When God got ready to start His work of
influencing the masses, He chose twelve men
who were most distinguished by their ignorance
Yet these men were destined to transform their
generation and all following ones.

The discovery of this treasure also brings you
wisdom. "But of him are you in Christ Jesus, who of
God is made unto us wisdom . . ." (I Corinthians
1:30).

The Bible says, "For it is written, I will destroy
the wisdom of the wise, and will bring to nothing the
understanding of the prudent. Where is the wise?
where is the scribe? where is the disputer of this
world? hath not God made foolish the wisdom of this
world? . . . . Because the foolishness of God is wiser
than men; and the weakness of God is stronger than
men. For you see your calling, brethren, how that not
many wise men after the flesh, not many mighty, not
many noble, are called: But God hath chosen the

foolish things of the world to confound the wise; and God hath chosen the weak things of the world to confound the things which are mighty; And base things of the world, and things which are despised, hath God chosen, yea, and things which are not, to bring to nought things that are: That no flesh should glory in his presence. But of him are you in Christ Jesus, who of God is made unto us wisdom, and righteousness, and sanctification, and redemption. That, according as it is written, He that glories, let him glory in the Lord" (I Corinthians 1:19-31).

Emerson, the man considered by some to be the greatest intellect in American history, knew a lot about philosophy, but nothing about calves. In his favorite story about himself, Emerson told about the day he and his son tried to get a large bull calf into a pen. They whistled and called, tugged and begged. The calf did not budge. Before giving up, the brilliant philosopher had his son take hold of the calf's ears and pull, with all his might while he was on the other end pushing with all his might. The calf still would not budge. He finally gave up, assuming there was no way they could get the calf in the pen.

Emerson heard a laugh and looked up to see a farm lady standing on her porch who was very amused by his futile attempts. She trotted down into the yard and stuck her finger in the calf's mouth. As soon as the calf started sucking, she gently moved into the pen, the calf following her; sucking on the finger all the way. Emerson said he had learned we were all ignorant, just about different things.

A little wisdom, a little know-how, can make impossible tasks very simple. It is true of calves. It is equally true with people. When God got ready to start His work of influencing the masses of people on this earth, He chose twelve men who were most distinguished by their ignorance (Acts 4:13). Yet these men were destined to transform their generation and all following ones. The key? The God of all wisdom was living inside them, "Christ Jesus, who of God is made unto us wisdom" (I Corinthians 1:30).

Jesus' fantastic wisdom

Jesus' wisdom in handling people was fantastic the day they dragged a woman before Him. They asked Him what should be done with a woman who had been caught in adultery. If Jesus had said, "Let her go," they would have said He was breaking Jewish law, for it commanded the stoning of such offenders. If He had said, "Stone her," they could have cried He was teaching insurrection against the Roman government, which forbid such executions. But Jesus was too wise. He said, "He that is without sin among you, let him first cast a stone at her" (John 8:7). All the Pharisee traps could not stop Jesus' influence.

Don't let being dumb
ever bother you again

Being a native of south Louisiana has created problems for me. South Louisiana is predominately Cajun. The French from Arcadia settled here. There are still many of us here who cannot read, write or even speak English. Everywhere I travel people asks, "Where are you from?" When I reply, "South Louisiana," they often say, "Oh, you are one of those dumb Cajuns." It was particularly embarrassing when a school president introduced me as being from South Louisiana and the audience snickered. But one day I read in the Bible that God hath "chosen the foolish things" (I Corinthians 1:27). I laughed as I said, "God, you ought to really be able to use somebody from south Louisiana!" Being dumb has never bothered me since. I have the God of all wisdom living inside my body.

My Daily Journal

On what date did you read this lesson ?_________
Study to show thyself approved unto God, a workman that needs not to be ashamed (2 Tim 2:15).

What Christ-like deed have you done?

____

____

Why do you call me Lord, Lord and not do the things that I say (Luke 6:46)?

Which temptations have you overcome?

____

____

Blessed is the man that endures temptation: for when he is tried, he shall receive the crown of life (James 1:12).

Which temptations have you yield to?

____

____

If we confess our sins, he is faithful and just to forgive us our sins, and to cleanse us from all unrighteousness (I John 1:9).

CHAPTER
TWENTY-NINE

THE WINNER'S WEALTH

*The poorest man I know is the man
who has nothing but money.
—John D. Rockefeller*

The discovery of this treasure—"CHRIST IN YOU"—will bring you the true wealth of a Winner. It brings power, peace of mind, constant joy, getting up in the morning with a sense of purpose, real love, achievements that will outlast the grave, a clean conscience, abiding confidence, and much more.

God has promised us this vast wealth: "That I may cause those that love me to inherit substance; and I will fill their treasures" (Proverbs 8:21). It is the will of God that your treasures should be full.

You must receive this. It is God's will for you to be rich in the true treasures: "The blessing of the Lord, it makes rich, and he adds no sorrow with it" (Proverbs 10:22).

The purpose of Jesus' mission into this world was to fulfill that purpose and make you rich: "For you know the grace of our Lord Jesus Christ, that, though he was rich, yet for your sakes He became poor, that you through his poverty might be rich" (II Corinthians

8:9). Jesus gave up all the riches of heaven and even gave up His life on a Roman cross that through His poverty we "might be rich." The cross towers over the ages reminding us that Jesus suffered and died that we would not have to live as paupers, but enjoy the real riches of life.

When Paul discovered the treasure of Christ living in his body, he referred to it as "the unsearchable riches of Christ" (Ephesians 3:8). Like a man who has just discovered his property contains a gold mine, he has only one problem. He's not going to live long enough to search out all the gold, to mine all there is. So he throws his arms in the air and exclaims, "Oh! Unsearchable riches!"

No man will live long enough to discover all the treasures in Christ. They are "unsearchable."

All that is gold does not glitter

The riches of Christ do not glitter like this world's gold, but they are of far greater value. They are the riches of this world's true Winners.

Bob Johnson, the treasure hunter, confided in me that his treasure had brought an endless chain of problems into his life. Huge taxes had to be paid, years of hard work had to be done, and legal battles had to be fought. But Bob said, "The discovery of Jesus Christ has been worth so much more to me than finding that gold and silver."

John D. Rockefeller Jr. said, "The poorest man I know is the man who has nothing but money." All that is gold does not glitter.

There are hidden riches, which do not catch men's eye but have far greater value than those things which allure most men.

The poor rich men

In books like *Think and Grow Rich*, one of the men most often used as an example of great success is Charles Schwab. Mr. Schwab worked for Andrew Carnegie in the steel business for an annual salary of a million dollars back in the days when such a salary was unheard of. Schwab became the president of the largest independent steel company. Success books are littered with illustrations from his "successful" life. There is, however, one part of Schwab's life that is strangely left out. He spent the last five years of his life dejected by absolute poverty. He died in bankruptcy. The many books and motivational messages relate Mr. Schwab's life, don't tell aspiring young men this part of the story.

In 1923 Mr. Schwab and eight other extremely successful financiers held a meeting in the Edgewater Beach Hotel in Chicago. Included in the group were: Samuel Insull, president of the largest utility company; Howard Hopson, the man who headed the largest gas company; Arthur Cotton, the outstanding wheat speculator; Richard Whitney, the distinguished president of the New York Stock Exchange; Albert Fall, who was a member of the president's cabinet; Leon Fraser, who headed the bank of international settlements; Jesse Livermore, who was known as the "bear" on Wall Street; and Iver Kruegar, who headed a great business monopoly.

Bill Bright points out in his booklet, *Jesus and the Intellectual,* that twenty-five years later: Schwab had died in bankruptcy, Samuel Insull had passed away as a fugitive from justice, broke and hiding in a foreign country; Howard Hopson had gone insane;

Arthur Cotton had died abroad insolvent; Richard Whitney had been shamed by serving time in Sing Sing; Albert Fall had been granted a pardon from the penitentiary so he could die at home; Jesse Livermore, Iver Kruegar and Leon Fraser had all committed suicide.

The Bible says, "The blessing of the Lord, it makes rich, and he adds no sorrow with it" (Proverbs 10:22). Those who search for the disappointing riches of this world will someday be disappointed. But those who search for the blessing of Jesus Christ find no sorrow in Him.

Eli Black was the middle-aged chairman of a billion-dollar corporation and a multimillionaire himself, yet he jumped forty-floors floors to his death. John Wesley White, the Canadian author, pointed out that seventy-nine millionaires committed suicide in one year in the United States.

My Daily Journal

On what date did you read this lesson ?_________
Study to show thyself approved unto God, a workman that needs not to be ashamed (2 Tim 2:15).

What Christ-like deed have you done?

____

____

Why do you call me Lord, Lord and not do the things that I say (Luke 6:46)?

Which temptations have you overcome?

____

____

Blessed is the man that endures temptation: for when he is tried, he shall receive the crown of life (James 1:12).

Which temptations have you yield to?

____

____

If we confess our sins, he is faithful and just to forgive us our sins, and to cleanse us from all unrighteousness (I John 1:9).

CHAPTER
THIRTY

THE TRUE RICHES

*"If therefore you have not been faithful
in the unrighteous mammon,
who will commit to your trust the true riches?"
—Luke 16:11*

The *London Times* could not have said it better: "Money is the article which may be used as a universal passport to everywhere except heaven and the universal provider of everything except happiness." Many men have discovered that the wealth of this world is nothing more than a shabby handout.

Paul wrote the young man Timothy to set his ambitions upon the greater wealth of godliness: "But godliness with contentment is great gain. But they that will be rich fall into temptation and a snare, and into many foolish and hurtful lusts, which drown men in destruction and perdition" (I Timothy 6:6, 9).

All that's gold does not glitter. There are true riches worth far more than money, that are not so obvious to human eyes. Jesus Christ said, "If therefore you have not been faithful in the unrighteous mammon, who will commit to your trust the true riches?" (Luke 16:11). There is money and then there are the "true riches." We must not confuse them.

The true treasures so often go undiscovered

The poor blind world cannot see the great comfort of having Christ living in you. Jesus said, "And I will pray the Father, and he shall give you another Comforter, that he may abide with you for ever; Even the Spirit of truth; whom the world cannot receive, because it sees him not, neither knows him: but you know him; for he dwells with you, and shall be in you. I will not leave you comfortless: I will come to you" (John 14:16-18). Jesus promised that, by His Spirit, He would come to us. He would live in us and comfort us through the trials of life. The masses of this "seeing is believing" world cannot receive Him. He does not "glitter" in their sight. And so they miss the Comforter. What a tragedy!

The masses of members in today's churches are just as blind to the riches of Christ. Jesus said to the church at Laodicea, "Because you say, I am rich, and increased with goods, and have need of nothing; and know not that you art wretched, and miserable, and poor, and blind, and naked: I counsel thee to buy of me gold tried in the fire, that you may be rich" (Revelations 3:17,18).

This church was located in a wealthy trade center. The treasurer's report said that they were rich and increased with goods. But God looked down and said, "You are poor, and not only that, you are blind. Too blind to see that you are poor, to know your utter lack of any wealth." He admonished them to buy of him gold tried in the fire. Jesus Christ went through the fires of Calvary, was purified and constitutes the real wealth, but a wealth which this church, like so many today, had never discovered.

The prayer of the apostle Paul was, "That the God of our Lord Jesus Christ, the Father of glory, may give unto you the spirit of wisdom and revelation in the knowledge of him: The eyes of your understanding being enlightened; that you may know what is the hope of his calling, and what the riches of the glory of his inheritance IN the saints" (Ephesians 1: 17, 18). Men need their eyes opened to that gold which does not glitter. They desperately need the riches of His glory "in the saints."

Poor King Jehoshaphat built ships to go to Ophir for gold. But his hopes were in vain. The ships were dashed to pieces on the rocks at Eziongeber. Jehoshaphat was left standing on the shore waiting for ships that never came in (I Kings 22:48).

Someday Jehoshaphat's disappointment will come to all men who set their affections upon money instead of the real treasures of peace, joy and power which come from having Christ living in you.

You can have instant wealth

Oswald Sanders admonishes us, "Remember that this is not an attainment slowly achieved but an obtainment instantly received." The moment we decide we would rather have Jesus than anything, the moment we turn from our sins and receive Jesus Christ, that moment God in all His fullness comes to dwell in our bodies. From that day forward it is never a matter of getting anything else, but only a matter of discovering the treasure that is in our heart. If you have never received Him, you can do it this moment.

Lay hold to this treasure by faith. Simply renounce your sins, asks the Father in heaven for forgiveness, and call upon Him to come into your heart. The scripture promises, "For whosoever shall call upon the name of the Lord shall be saved" (Romans 10:13).

File your claim

If you have already received Christ, then begin filing claims to the treasure that is yours. That's the way treasure hunters do it. They rush into the government's offices and file their claims. A man may study the maps and correctly locate great treasures. He may even dive into the ocean and gaze on the gold. But until he stands before a government representative and files an official claim, he will never have a legal claim to one cent of it.

Likewise, Christians may spend their life reading the Bible, delighting in the wealth that Christ offers, but they will never actually possess any of it until they stand before God and file a claim. They must boldly declare, "I have received Christ; all the Bible promises is mine." I claim it as my own.

Take hold of God's promises and say, "God promised me this treasure in Christ. I have received Jesus into my heart; therefore His peace, His joy, His power and His life are mine!" Paul filed his claim, boldly declaring, "It is no longer I but Christ that lives in me" (Galatians 2:20). Then Paul was transformed from a hateful, vicious killer into the humble apostle who would lead a world to a better life.

Don't ever live like a pauper again. Don't ever feel inferior to any human being. If Jesus Christ lives in you, you have all things. You are wealthy beyond all expression. You can anticipate spending the rest of your days discovering treasures and filing claim to them.

The discovery that Jesus Christ is living in your heart is the greatest of all life's discoveries. It transforms your life as nothing else possibly can. It changes you, and changes you, and changes you, and keeps on changing you. It is life's transforming discovery.

My Daily Journal

On what date did you read this lesson ?__________
Study to show thyself approved unto God, a workman that needs not to be ashamed (2 Tim 2:15).

What Christ-like deed have you done?

____

____

Why do you call me Lord, Lord and not do the things that I say (Luke 6:46)?

Which temptations have you overcome?

____

____

Blessed is the man that endures temptation: for when he is tried, he shall receive the crown of life (James 1:12).

Which temptations have you yield to?

____

____

If we confess our sins, he is faithful and just to forgive us our sins, and to cleanse us from all unrighteousness (I John 1:9).

CHAPTER
THIRTY-ONE

LIVE IN NEED
OF NOTHING

I Am—thy Peace, thy Joy,
Thy Righteousness, thy Might;
I Am—thy Victory o'er sin,
Thy Keeper day and night.
—*Adah Richmond*

This discovery of Christ living in you gives you "all riches" (Colossians 2:2). Colossians 3:11 declares: "Christ is all, and in all." Now if Christ is "all," the embodiment of all worthwhile treasures, and He's in all that believe, then it means we have "all." We must, therefore, conclude with Paul that we "are complete in him" (Colossians 2:10).

An astonishing discovery, isn't it? From the moment you received Christ Jesus, the God of all patience, all power, all joy, all love, all peace and all victory has lived inside your body! That is the greatest treasure discovery of all ages.

Adab Richmond discovered
he was complete in Christ

"CHRIST WHO IS OUR LIFE"

"I AM." Who art You, Lord?
I Am—all things to thee;
Sufficient to thine every need;
You art complete in Me.

I Am—thy Peace, thy Joy,
Thy Righteousness, thy Might;
I Am—thy Victory o'er sin,
Thy Keeper day and night.

I Am—thy Way, thy Life;
I Am—thy Life within,
I Am—the Word of Truth;
Thine Everlasting Bread;
Whate'er thy lack, I Am—to thee
Eat of my Flesh, drink of my Blood,
El Shaddai, Enough.
I Am—what dost you need?
—*Adah Richmond*

My Daily Journal

On what date did you read this lesson ?__________
Study to show thyself approved unto God, a workman that needs not to be ashamed (2 Tim 2:15).

What Christ-like deed have you done?
____

____

Why do you call me Lord, Lord and not do the things that I say (Luke 6:46)?

Which temptations have you overcome?
____

____

Blessed is the man that endures temptation: for when he is tried, he shall receive the crown of life (James 1:12).

Which temptations have you yield to?
____

____

If we confess our sins, he is faithful and just to forgive us our sins, and to cleanse us from all unrighteousness (I John 1:9).

CHAPTER
THIRTY-TWO

LET THE SUBMARINE'S SECRET WORK FOR YOU

Even "men of steel" fold unless there is a pressure within them greater than the pressure outside them.

If you want to succeed in life, you must not miss the secret of the submarine. They plunge to the ocean's depths and are subjected to tons of pressure. They endure it successfully as long as they maintain internal pressure equal to the outside pressure. If they depressurize, the submarine collapses like a paper cup. The strength of the steel is never adequate. It is the "unseen" internal pressure that enables the vessel to successfully endure the ocean's depths.

You are pressurized to survive

The submarine's key can work for you. Your life will be subject to fantastic pressures. Even "men of steel" fold unless there is an unseen pressure inside them greater than the pressures outside them. But you can be "pressurized" to survive anything. "You are of God, little children. I have overcome them: because greater is he that is in you, than he that is in the world" (I John 4:4).

Withstand the fear of death

There is no pressure ever put on people greater than the threat of death. Self-preservation is basic. When God called Stephen to confront the hypocritical religious leaders of his day, he knew they would probably kill him. The pressure to compromise was on. But he boldly stood before them and declared, "You stiffnecked and uncircumcised in heart and ears, you do always resist the Holy Ghost: as your fathers did, so do you" (Acts 7:51). They stoned him to death. After watching this, one of his assassins was converted and became the great apostle Paul.

Withstand the pressure to compromise

How could Stephen resist the pressure to compromise and escape death? It was only because he was "full of faith and power" (Acts 6:8). There is an enemy out there—the devil. He is tempting you to compromise in business, to yield to sexual allurement, to succumb to the habit of alcohol, to cheat, to lie, to steal, to hate, to be jealous, greedy, or unforgiving. The pressure he puts upon you is too great. You will collapse and fold up unless . . . unless you discover the secret of pressurization which is "Christ in you." Once you have made that discovery you can take anything, "because greater is he that is in you, than he that is in the world" (I John 4:4).

Withstand the pressure of anger

The life of Paul Kirkendall is one of the world's great success stories. A former gambler, conartist, and strong-arm man, Paul received Jesus Christ and later became a preacher and director of a great rescue mission in Blytheville, Arkansas. Paul keeps an assortment of liquor, wine, pistols, dice, etc., on display in his study. When I asked him why, he said, "In case I ever meet anyone greater than the One who is in me, I won't have to go out and look for it." But the liquor, guns, and dice remain on the shelves year after year. Paul Kirkendall never met a temptation more powerful than the One who was in him.

Wise Solomon wrote: "He that is slow to anger is better than the mighty; and he that rules his spirit than he that takes a city" (Proverbs 16:32). If you rule a city, and yet passion rules you, you are poor indeed. Our weakness is a paradox. "Behold, we put bits in the horses' mouths, that they may obey us; and we turn about their whole body. Behold also the ships, which though they be so great, and are driven of fierce winds, yet are they turned about with a very small helm, wherever the governor listeth. For every kind of beasts, and of birds, and of serpents, and of things in the sea, is tamed, of mankind: But the tongue can no man tame; it is an unruly evil" (James 3:3, 4, 7, 8). It can wreck you if it isn't controlled. Yet no man can tame it. Only God.

And how important is the control of our tongues? Well, you remember an American president was forced from office because he had the power to rule an empire but couldn't control his tongue!

You don't have to live like that. Don't let passion rule you another day. Claim your treasure. By God's power in your heart, master your fate. Rule over your mind and body. Discipline yourself down the narrow road to success.

My Daily Journal

On what date did you read this lesson ?________

Study to show thyself approved unto God, a workman that needs not to be ashamed (2 Tim 2:15).

What Christ-like deed have you done?

____

____

Why do you call me Lord, Lord and not do the things that I say (Luke 6:46)?

Which temptations have you overcome?

____

____

Blessed is the man that endures temptation: for when he is tried, he shall receive the crown of life (James 1:12).

Which temptations have you yield to?

____

____

If we confess our sins, he is faithful and just to forgive us our sins, and to cleanse us from all unrighteousness (I John 1:9).

CHAPTER
THIRTY-THREE

BECOME A CHAMPION OF PERSEVERING PATIENCE

**The God living within us
is the God of all patience.**

A lady once asked a minister I know to pray for her. She said, "My husband and I are real Christians. We go to church, give our money and work for the Lord. But we have a problem. Please pray for God to give us patience." The minister replied, "No, I wouldn't pray for you." The astonished lady said, "You are joking." He replied, "I've never been more serious in my life." She asked, "Well, why wouldn't you pray for me to have patience?" He answered, "You told me you are a Christian and that means Christ lives in your heart. Now Romans 15:5 says, 'Now the God of patience and consolation grant you to be likeminded one toward another according to Christ Jesus.' The God who lives within us is 'the God of all patience.' He lives within us to make us likeminded, or patient, with others. What you need is not to get patience. You need to discover the patience God has already given you. God is no dispenser of graces, sitting up in heaven to give you a little patience. He meets all your needs in Christ."

Watchman Nee puts it this way: "It is not that I have strength through Him to seek humility, meekness, holiness (or patience). He is all that in me; for He is my Life. The Christian has not a lot of odds and ends of virtues; indeed, he has no virtues; he just has Christ. The question is again, do we believe God's Word? Do we believe I Corinthians 1:30?" The passage says the God living within us is the God of all patience. Therefore we can file a claim on patience, and it becomes ours!

My Daily Journal

On what date did you read this lesson ?_______
Study to show thyself approved unto God, a workman that needs not to be ashamed (2 Tim 2:15).

What Christ-like deed have you done?

____

____

Why do you call me Lord, Lord and not do the things that I say (Luke 6:46)?

Which temptations have you overcome?

____

____

Blessed is the man that endures temptation: for when he is tried, he shall receive the crown of life (James 1:12).

Which temptations have you yield to?

____

____

If we confess our sins, he is faithful and just to forgive us our sins, and to cleanse us from all unrighteousness (I John 1:9).

CHAPTER
THIRTY-FOUR

STOP STRUGGLING AND START SUCCEEDING

*It is wonderful that God is not
limited to our abilities.
He can live His life in us and
work His influence through us.*

A man struggles to achieve happiness, to find some noble purpose for living, to escape death. But through the years he feels himself slipping. The guilt piles up, happiness begins to diminish, death becomes a more startling reality. He loses confidence in his own abilities. Day by day he seems to sink lower and lower in despair. But the whole vicious slide can be interrupted. There can be a day in a man's life when he discovers Christ living in him. From that day forward he reverses the downward spiral and starts moving up in life. No longer is he struggling with life alone. It is Christ living in him. The moment that happens, his whole life is changed. The downward slide is forever reversed.

God is not limited by
our talents or experience

In Prairieville, Louisiana, I once saw the miracle power of Jesus Christ living in a human body. A timid little lady by the name of Mrs. Don Hudson was very concerned about some friends whose conduct she did not approve of. She was growing increasingly frustrated because she felt she could not do anything about it.

One morning I spoke on the subject of "Jesus Christ Living in You" at the little mission church she attended there in the French country of south Louisiana. Mrs. Hudson listened. When I invited the people to meet and then go out and visit other people, she came. But Mrs. Hudson warned me she was too timid to talk to anyone.

I said, "Mrs. Hudson, doesn't Jesus Christ have all the power and wisdom in the universe?" . . . . "Yes," she replied. "And doesn't Jesus Christ live inside you" I asked. Again she replied, "Yes." I said, "Well, don't worry about it, just trust the Lord to do it through you."

I never did get her convinced, but I got her in the car. That night, among the seven converts, there was a young married couple.

Mrs. Hudson came running up to me after the service. She was crying and weeping at the same time. "See that couple that received Christ," she said. "Yes," I replied. "Well, that is the first visit I ever made for Jesus!"

She related, "I talked with the lady a few minutes. Everything was going well until I got the Bible out and started to read it. I got scared and choked up. I couldn't say a word. Then, remembering what you had said, I bowed my head and told the Lord He was in me and asked Him to help me win the lady to Jesus. Then I opened my mouth . . . and nothing came out!

"I was so upset I knew I was going to cry. I didn't want her to see me, so I knelt down by her couch and buried my face. Then it happened. Something bumped me. I looked up and that lady was kneeling down beside me and she was crying too.

"I never did talk to her. We just knelt there and cried a while and tonight she came to Christ—Isn't that wonderful!"

Well, Mrs. Don Hudson never did get to where she could talk to people, but before that week's meeting was over, she had cried three families to the Lord! Mrs. Hudson had discovered the Winner within her. Her life spiraled upward from that moment.

It is wonderful that God is not limited to our abilities. He can live His life in us and work His influence through us.

My Daily Journal

On what date did you read this lesson ?________

Study to show thyself approved unto God, a workman that needs not to be ashamed (2 Tim 2:15).

What Christ-like deed have you done?

____

____

Why do you call me Lord, Lord and not do the things that I say (Luke 6:46)?

Which temptations have you overcome?

____

____

Blessed is the man that endures temptation: for when he is tried, he shall receive the crown of life (James 1:12).

Which temptations have you yield to?

____

____

If we confess our sins, he is faithful and just to forgive us our sins, and to cleanse us from all unrighteousness (I John 1:9).

CHAPTER
THIRTY-FIVE

THE POWER
TO SUCCEED

**And remember, nuclear power
has been available all the time.
It is everywhere. But man just
hadn't discovered it.**

There is a discovery that fills the weakest person with the power to succeed. I am not talking of athletic power to run through football lines or political power to influence decisions. I am talking of a far greater power than that. I am talking about power to go through adversity; power to succeed under impossible circumstances; power to control your own life; power to influence other people, power to endure until your goal is reached.

All power in heaven and earth
can be yours

Jesus Christ declared, "All power is given unto me in heaven and in earth" (Matthew 28:18) and the moment we receive Him, this Christ of "all power" dwells in our hearts. Think of it—God was powerful enough to create one hundred thousand galaxies of stars. By His might He moves giant planets at will.

God imparted enough power to just a few pounds of uranium to blow up a nation and the power inside the atom was placed there by the same God that lives in our hearts. Jewish prophet Micah cried out, "But truly I am full of power by the spirit of the Lord" (Micah 3:8).

A man complained to me, "I am just too weak." I said, "Praise God, Brother! That qualifies you to become the strongest man living." God said to a weakened Paul, "My strength is made perfect in weakness" (II Corinthians 12:9). The weaker you are, the more you have to depend on God's strength. Paul discovered this and shouted, "For when I am weak, then I am strong" (II Corinthians 12:10). The weaker you are, the more glory God gets out of succeeding through you. "God hath chosen the weak things of the world to confound the things which are mighty . . . That no flesh should glory in his presence" (I Corinthians 1:27, 29).

Are you weak? Then you are a candidate for the world's strongest person. There is no one for you to trust but God. There will be no one to get the glory but God. You are just what heaven is searching for!

My Daily Journal

On what date did you read this lesson ?_________

Study to show thyself approved unto God, a workman that needs not to be ashamed (2 Tim 2:15).

What Christ-like deed have you done?

____

____

Why do you call me Lord, Lord and not do the things that I say (Luke 6:46)?

Which temptations have you overcome?

____

____

Blessed is the man that endures temptation: for when he is tried, he shall receive the crown of life (James 1:12).

Which temptations have you yield to?

____

____

If we confess our sins, he is faithful and just to forgive us our sins, and to cleanse us from all unrighteousness (I John 1:9).

CHAPTER
THIRTY-SIX

WHEN YOUR STRENGTH ENDS, GOD'S BEGINS

"A drowning man cannot be saved until he is utterly exhausted, and ceases to make the slightest effort to save himself.
—Watchman Nee

Watchman Nee, who died in a Communist prison, once said, "I was once staying in a place in China with some twenty other brothers. There was inadequate provision for bathing in the home where we stayed, so we went for a daily plunge in the river. On one occasion a brother had a cramp in one leg, and I suddenly saw he was sinking fast, so I motioned to another brother, who was an expert swimmer, to hasten to his rescue. But to my astonishment he made no move. So I grew desperate and called out: 'Don't you see the man is drowning?' and the other brothers, about as agitated as I was, shouted vigorously too. But our good swimmer still did not move. Calm and collected, he remained just where he was, apparently postponing the unwelcome task. Meantime the voice of the poor, drowning brother grew fainter and his efforts feebler. In my heart I said: 'I hate that man!' Think of his letting a brother drown before his very eyes and not going to the rescue!'

"But when the man was actually sinking, with a few swift strokes the swimmer was at his side, and both were safely ashore. When I got an opportunity I aired my views. 'I have never seen any Christian who loved his life quite as much as you do', I said. 'Think of the distress you would have saved that brother if you had considered yourself a little less and him a little more.' But the swimmer knew his business better than I did. 'Had I gone earlier', he said,' he would have clutched me so fast that both of us would have gone under. A drowning man cannot be saved until he is utterly exhausted, and ceases to make the slightest effort to save himself.'"

This is the key to the winning life. God is waiting for us to exhaust our strength, to come to the end of ourselves. Then He is able to become our strength and our life.

Lifelong power

The power of Christ in the heart of man lasts a life time. It begins in youth and it goes through old age. The Psalmist declares the strength Christ gave in youth: Many a time have they afflicted me from my youth: yet they have not prevailed against me (Psalms 129:2).

The Psalmist declared the power of God remained even when he was old. That power transformed his old age from a time of failing strength to fantastic spiritual power. It gave him a wonderful purpose in his last days, "Now also when I am old and gray-headed, O God, forsake me not; until I have showed thy strength unto this generation, and thy power to every one that is to come" (Psalm 71:18).

Showing youth the riches of God's power in him whips the old man's twilight years into an exciting time!

My Daily Journal

On what date did you read this lesson ?_________

Study to show thyself approved unto God, a workman that needs not to be ashamed (2 Tim 2:15).

What Christ-like deed have you done?

____

____

Why do you call me Lord, Lord and not do the things that I say (Luke 6:46)?

Which temptations have you overcome?

____

____

Blessed is the man that endures temptation: for when he is tried, he shall receive the crown of life (James 1:12).

Which temptations have you yield to?

____

____

If we confess our sins, he is faithful and just to forgive us our sins, and to cleanse us from all unrighteousness (I John 1:9).

CHAPTER
THIRTY-SEVEN

———

NUCLEAR POWER WAS ALWAYS HERE, WAITING ON MEN TO DISCOVER IT

"The eyes of your understanding being enlightened; that you may know . . . what is the exceeding greatness of his power toward us who believe, according to the working of his mighty power"
—Ephesians 1:18, 19

Power! That is the treasure. Power is the difference between rowing a Viking boat through the Atlantic and slicing through the water in a nuclear vessel. And remember, nuclear power has been available all the time. It is everywhere. But man just hadn't discovered it. Do not be affected by public opinion. Most people see no power in Christ. But nobody saw any power in the atom!

Don't flounder around another day in a pitiful weak life. Discover your treasure. With "the eyes of your understanding being enlightened; that you may know . . . what is the exceeding greatness of his power toward us who believe, according to the working of his mighty power" (Ephesians 1:18, 19).

Realize that "it is God which works in you both to will and to do" (Philippians 2:13).

Open your mouth and declare as Isaiah did: "My God shall be my strength" (Isaiah 49:5). No more weakness. "My God shall be my strength." Declare it boldly. "My God shall be my strength."

My Daily Journal

On what date did you read this lesson ?_______

Study to show thyself approved unto God, a workman that needs not to be ashamed (2 Tim 2:15).

What Christ-like deed have you done?

____

____

Why do you call me Lord, Lord and not do the things that I say (Luke 6:46)?

Which temptations have you overcome?

____

Blessed is the man that endures temptation: for when he is tried, he shall receive the crown of life (James 1:12).

Which temptations have you yield to?

____

If we confess our sins, he is faithful and just to forgive us our sins, and to cleanse us from all unrighteousness (I John 1:9).

CHAPTER
THIRTY-EIGHT

FREE YOUR LIFE
FROM WORRY

Suddenly, something happened . . . I felt the
power of God. From that day to this,
my life has been free from worry.
—J. C. Penney

I never pass a Penney's store without getting excited. On April 14, 1902, J. C. Penney, a young man with five hundred dollars, started his business. When the depression hit in 1929 J. C. Penney's business crashed.

Harassed with worries, he developed the painful illness of shingles. The doctor's treatment did not help. Day by day he became weaker. Penney was physically and mentally exhausted. He despaired. He felt he didn't have a friend left in the world.

One night Dr. Eggleston gave him a sedative. He went to sleep with the overwhelming conviction that it was his last night on earth.

To his surprise he survived the night. When he awoke he could hear a choir from a nearby chapel singing, "God will take care of you." Penney said, "Suddenly, something happened. I can't explain it. I can only call it a miracle. I felt as if I had been instantly lifted out of the darkness of a dungeon into warm, brilliant sunlight. I felt the power of God. From that day to this, my life has been free from worry."

Before his death Penney saw his stores become the largest chain of dry good, stores in the world. But the entrance of God's power and peace brought him far greater wealth than any of his cash registers.

My Daily Journal

On what date did you read this lesson ?_________
Study to show thyself approved unto God, a workman that needs not to be ashamed (2 Tim 2:15).

What Christ-like deed have you done?

____

____

Why do you call me Lord, Lord and not do the things that I say (Luke 6:46)?

Which temptations have you overcome?

____

____

Blessed is the man that endures temptation: for when he is tried, he shall receive the crown of life (James 1:12).

Which temptations have you yield to?

____

____

If we confess our sins, he is faithful and just to forgive us our sins, and to cleanse us from all unrighteousness (I John 1:9).

CHAPTER
THIRTY-NINE

HOW TO OVERCOME YOUR OPPOSITION

*"I kept saying one thing over and over.
I kept repeating it even when I got too weak
to understand what the words meant,
'I can do all things through Christ
which strengthens me.'"*
— Howard Rutledge

People will turn against you if you attempt to succeed at anything: building a home, a church, a business, or developing a skill. The more successful you become, the more persecution you will have.

Stop and compare your opponents with those of Howard Rutledge. Howard believed it was God's will for him to be a military officer. He ambitiously sought to succeed. One day, as he was methodically climbing the ranks to the top of his profession, it all fell in.

Howard Rutledge won after six years of communist torture

Howard Rutledge was shot down over Vietnam.

The Communists threw him in a cell with no bed. They shut him up in solitary confinement. What little food he got was hardly fit to eat. There was no doctor and no medical treatment.

Rutledge had done his best to succeed, but other human beings were subjecting him to hunger, pain, loneliness, terror, persecution, and the constant possibility of death.

When we had dinner together in San Diego, Howard told me he got too weak to even knock the huge rats off when they crawled around on his body.

This torture went on for six long hopeless years. I asked him, "Howard, how in the world did you come through it?" "Moody," he replied, "there was only one way I made it. I kept saying one thing over and over. I kept repeating it even when I got too weak to understand what the words meant, 'I can do all things through Christ which strengthens me'" (Philippians 4:13).

Howard Rutledge was freed and reunited with his family. They wrote a book on his life and made a movie of it: *In The Presence Of Mine Enemies*. He was promoted and reassigned to the Philippines.

Other men could not stop this man. Christ was in him. Christ strengthened him. By the power of God he overcame all his enemies.

My Daily Journal

On what date did you read this lesson ?______

Study to show thyself approved unto God, a workman that needs not to be ashamed (2 Tim 2:15).

What Christ-like deed have you done?

____

____

Why do you call me Lord, Lord and not do the things that I say (Luke 6:46)?

Which temptations have you overcome?

____

____

Blessed is the man that endures temptation: for when he is tried, he shall receive the crown of life (James 1:12).

Which temptations have you yield to?

____

____

If we confess our sins, he is faithful and just to forgive us our sins, and to cleanse us from all unrighteousness (I John 1:9).

**CHAPTER
FORTY**

SURVIVING A BROKEN HEART

**"It is God that avenges me"
—David**

Howard Rutledge was persecuted by alien enemies—by Communists. Perhaps you have had your family or closest friends turn against you. That was what happened to a Bible lad named David.

He loved Saul. David loyally served Saul. But Saul became jealous of him and sent armies to kill him. But David, hiding in a cave and hunted by an army of friends, declared his faith, "I shall not be moved." That faith not only carried him through the persecution; it carried him all the way to the throne. David became king.

What goes on inside a man like this? After his great victory, David documented his secret of success like this: "And David spoke unto the Lord the words of this song in the day that the Lord had delivered him out of the hand of all his enemies, and out of the hand of Saul: And he said, 'The Lord is my . . . deliverer . . . For by thee I have run through a troop . . . God is my strength and power . . . you have girded me with strength to battle: them that rose up against me have you subdued under me . . . It is God that avenges me, and that brings down the people under me, and . . . have lifted me up on high above them that rose against me'" (II Samuel 22:1, 2, 30, 33, 40, 48, 49).

That is your key to overcoming opposition. David declared, "God is my strength," and God lifted him above the many who were trying to kill him. That same God wants to live inside your body, strengthen you, and exalt you over all who break your heart!

My Daily Journal

On what date did you read this lesson ?________
Study to show thyself approved unto God, a workman that needs not to be ashamed (2 Tim 2:15).

What Christ-like deed have you done?
____
____

Why do you call me Lord, Lord and not do the things that I say (Luke 6:46)?

Which temptations have you overcome?
____
____

Blessed is the man that endures temptation: for when he is tried, he shall receive the crown of life (James 1:12).

Which temptations have you yield to?
____
____

If we confess our sins, he is faithful and just to forgive us our sins, and to cleanse us from all unrighteousness (I John 1:9).

CHAPTER
FORTY-ONE

SUCCEED THROUGH SELF-CONTROL

"Lord this is Your affair; I count on You.
The victory is Yours, and You, not I,
shall have the credit."
—Watchman Nee

Though you may be very weak, the Winner within you is able to overcome any temptation you face. This is vital to any successful life. Temptations are many and might. They destroy masses of people's homes, business, and lives. The demonic lusts for sex, drugs, power, money and vengeance enslave their captives. Jesus spoke of the victims as those who, "in time of temptation fall away" (Luke 8:13).

But amidst all the threatening temptations God promises we can win: "There hath no temptation taken you but such as is common to man: but God is faithful, who will not suffer you to be tempted above that you are able; but will with the temptation also make a way to escape, that you may be able to bear it" (I Corinthians 10:13).

But God not only tells us we can overcome

temptation. He gives the power to win. He comes to live within us, enabling us to declare: "You are of God, little children, and have overcome them: because greater is he that is in you, than he that is in the world" (I John 4:4).

When you are the weakest, you become the strongest

Watchman Nee points out the difference between the person who has discovered the Winner within and the one who hasn't. The ones who haven't are struggling: "Oh yes, we know we should have victory, so when we meet with a temptation we take great care, and we watch, and we pray. We feel it is our duty to fight against that thing, and to reject it, so we make up our minds not to do so, exerting our wills to the utmost. But that is not our victory. Christ is our victory. We do not need will power and determination to resist the tempter. We look to Him who is our life. 'Lord, this is Your affair; I count on You. The victory is Yours, and You, not I, shall have the credit.' So often we gain a kind of victory, and everyone knows about it! We achieved it ourselves; but communion is broken and there is no peace.

"Many of us live in constant fear of temptation. We know just how much we can stand, but alas, we have not discovered how much Christ can stand. 'I can stand temptation up to a point, but beyond that point, I am done for.'

"There are, on the one hand, some very strong, almost extreme words in Scripture. 'God . . . always leads us in triumph.' 'Sin shall not have dominion over you.' 'To me to live is Christ.' 'I can do all things through Christ.'

"They are bold, strong, almost boastful affirmations. Yet the same people who say these things must also say: 'I was with you in weakness, and in fear, and in much trembling.' 'I am chief of sinners.' (Note there the present tense in the Greek.) 'We have no hope in ourselves.' 'The blood of Jesus his Son cleanses us from all sin.' 'If we say that we have no sin, we deceive ourselves.' 'We also are weak in him.' 'When I am weak, then am I strong.' 'Most gladly therefore will I rather glory in my weaknesses.'"[5]

My Daily Journal

On what date did you read this lesson ?_________
Study to show thyself approved unto God, a workman that needs not to be ashamed (2 Tim 2:15).

What Christ-like deed have you done?

____

____

Why do you call me Lord, Lord and not do the things that I say (Luke 6:46)?

Which temptations have you overcome?

____

Blessed is the man that endures temptation: for when he is tried, he shall receive the crown of life (James 1:12).

Which temptations have you yield to?

____

If we confess our sins, he is faithful and just to forgive us our sins, and to cleanse us from all unrighteousness (I John 1:9).

CHAPTER
FORTY-TWO

THE WAY TO WIN
OVER TEMPTATION

"Instead of fighting against bad temper, he (Lord Radstock) took Christ to be his patience, his humility, his meekness, his self-control. "
—F. B. Meyer

Author F. B. Meyer relates this conversation with Lord Radstock in which he related how he overcame anger. Radstock said, "I used once to be overcome by temper. I fought against temper. I came to the end of myself one afternoon when a number of children refused to listen to my teaching. I was on the point of losing my temper, when I turned to Christ, and said, 'Christ, be my sweet temper.'"

Meyer said, "Instead of fighting against bad temper, he took Christ to be his patience, his humility, his meekness, his self-control. I saw in a moment that it was a better experience.

"From that moment I have tried to live that way, and whatever I have needed, I have said, 'Christ, be this in me.'

Discover the Winner within you and you can

overcome all temptations. Because He lives in you, you can overcome temptations. File your claim on victory over temptation and look forward to your great reward: "Blessed is the man that endures temptation: for when he is tried, he shall receive the crown of life, which the Lord hath promised to them that love him" (James 1:12).

My Daily Journal

On what date did you read this lesson ?________
Study to show thyself approved unto God, a workman that needs not to be ashamed (2 Tim 2:15).

What Christ-like deed have you done?

____

____

Why do you call me Lord, Lord and not do the things that I say (Luke 6:46)?

Which temptations have you overcome?

____

____

Blessed is the man that endures temptation: for when he is tried, he shall receive the crown of life (James 1:12).

Which temptations have you yield to?

____

____

If we confess our sins, he is faithful and just to forgive us our sins, and to cleanse us from all unrighteousness (I John 1:9).

CHAPTER
FORTY-THREE

MAKING SURE
YOU WILL
NEVER GIVE UP

There is a limit to how long
a mortal can keep on pushing.
But there is no limit to how long
Jesus Christ can keep pushing.

Even winning can become tiresome. The years can beat a person down. The leading runners can faint. There is a limit to how long a mortal can keep on pushing. But there is no limit to how long Jesus Christ can keep pushing.

God's Word says, don't give up, but look to the Winner within you: "Wherefore seeing we also are compassed about with so great a cloud of witnesses, let us lay aside every weight, and the sin which does so easily beset us, and let us run with patience the race that is set before us, Looking unto Jesus the author and finisher of our faith; who for the joy that was set before him endured the cross, despising the shame, and is set down at the right hand of the throne of God. For consider him that endured such contradiction of sinners against himself, lest you be wearied and faint in your minds" (Hebrews 12:1-3).

The power to persevere

"Have you not known? have you not heard, that the everlasting God, the Lord, the Creator of the ends of the earth, faints not, neither is weary? . . . He gives power to the faint; and to them that have no might he increases strength. Even the youths shall faint and be weary, and the young men shall utterly fall: But they that wait upon the Lord shall renew their strength; they shall mount up with wings as eagles; they shall run, and not be weary; and they shall walk, and not faint" (Isaiah 40:28-31).

With Jesus Christ living in your heart, you have a never failing power source. The God that dwells in our hearts never faints. He never grows weary. He never quits giving His power to the faint. He never ceases to increase the strength of those with no might.

Jacov Riis said, "When nothing seems to help, I go and look at a stonecutter, hammering away at his rock, perhaps a hundred times without as much as a crack showing in it. Yet at the hundred and first blow it will split in two, and I know it was not that blow that did it but all that had gone before." You have the right to claim the perseverance of a stonecutter.

Perseverance won over
the mighty Roman Empire

The apostle Peter wrote to warn persecuted Christians scattered throughout five Roman providences (I Peter 1:1). In just a very short while the government was to impose such fiery trials upon them that mere mortals could scarcely endure:

"Beloved, think it not strange concerning the fiery trial which is to try you, as though some strange thing happened unto you: But rejoice, inasmuch as you are partakers of Christ's sufferings; that, when his glory shall be revealed, you may be glad also with exceeding joy. If you be reproached for the name of Christ, happy are you; for the spirit of glory and of God rests upon you: on their part he is evil spoken of, but on your part he is glorified" (I Peter 4:12-14).

But Peter assured them they would be "kept by the power of God": "Blessed be the God and Father of our Lord Jesus Christ, which according to his abundant mercy hath begotten us again unto a lively hope by the resurrection of Jesus Christ from the dead, To an inheritance incorruptible, and undefiled, and that fades not away, reserved in heaven for you, Who are kept by the power of God through faith unto salvation ready to be revealed in the last time.

Wherein you greatly rejoice, though now for a season, if need be, you are in heaviness through manifold temptations: That the trial of your faith, being much more precious than of gold that perishes, though it be tried with fire, might be found unto praise and honors and glory at the appearing of Jesus Christ: Whom having not seen, you love; in whom, though now you see him not, yet believing, you rejoice with joy unspeakable and full of glory: Receiving the end of your faith, even the salvation of your souls" (I Peter 1:3-9).

And history records they were kept by the power of the Spirit within them. Rome accused them, burned them, tortured them and stripped them of every thing. But finally Rome ran out of power, died and passed into the sea of oblivion. But the Christians kept marching on triumphantly. They were kept by the power of God.

Claim your perseverance today

Claim your treasure! With Christ in your heart you have the power to persevere. Obstacles, handicaps, persecutions nor weariness can defeat you with Christ in your heart! File your official claim to the power to persevere. Open your mouth and declare with the Psalmist, "I will go in the strength of the Lord God" (Psalms 71:16) and go in that strength for the rest of your days. I will not give up!

My Daily Journal

On what date did you read this lesson ?______

Study to show thyself approved unto God, a workman that needs not to be ashamed (2 Tim 2:15).

What Christ-like deed have you done?

____

____

Why do you call me Lord, Lord and not do the things that I say (Luke 6:46)?

Which temptations have you overcome?

____

____

Blessed is the man that endures temptation: for when he is tried, he shall receive the crown of life (James 1:12).

Which temptations have you yield to?

____

____

If we confess our sins, he is faithful and just to forgive us our sins, and to cleanse us from all unrighteousness (I John 1:9).

**CHAPTER
FORTY-FOUR**

BECOME A
POSITIVE INFLUENCE

"I know men; and I tell you that Jesus Christ is no mere man. Between Him and every other person in the world there is no possible term of comparison. Alexander, Caesar, Charlemagne and I have founded empires. But on what did we rest the creations of our genius? Upon force. Jesus Christ founded His empire upon love, and at this hour millions of men would die for Him." — *Napoleon Bonaparte*

The most influential person that ever lived was Jesus Christ. It is quite reasonable that if Jesus Christ lives within you, you should therefore have great influence upon other people. Just consider the powerful impact the Winner within you made on people.

Napoleon Bonaparte confessed, "I know men; and I tell you that Jesus Christ is no mere man. Between Him and every other person in the world there is no possible term of comparison. Alexander, Caesar, Charlemagne and I have founded empires. But on what did we rest the creations of our genius? Upon force. Jesus Christ founded His Empire upon love, and at this hour millions of men would die for Him."

Sholem Asch, a Jew, said, "Jesus Christ is the outstanding personality of all time. No other teacher—Jewish, Christian, Buddhist, Mohammed—is still a teacher whose teaching is such a guidepost for the world we live in. He became the Light of the World. Why shouldn't I, a Jew, be proud of that."

The most unlikely person had the greatest influence on mankind

Life magazine stated, "Jesus gave history a new beginning. In every land He is at home: everywhere men think His face is like their best face—and like God's face. His birthday is kept across the world. His death-day has set a marker against 'every city skyline.'

"Jesus Christ not only was the most influential person who ever lived but was also the least likely person to influence others. He did not have the glamour of a sex symbol, His only romance was with the souls of men. He did not have wealth to allure men, He had to borrow a coin to illustrate a sermon.

"Jesus never held a position that would demand any respect. Jesus Christ never used flattery; His straightforward words stripped the hearts of men. Jesus never evaded a stand on issues, as to allow men to think He sided with them when He did not. Yet this blunt, controversial, poor man, without position, has effected a greater influence upon a greater number of people for a greater length of time than any man who ever lived!"

You may not possess any of the attributes that the world thinks are essential to being a great leader. You may hold no position. You may feel like a very small, unimportant person. Yet, with Jesus Christ living inside of you, you have unlimited potential for influencing other humans.

My Daily Journal

On what date did you read this lesson ?________
Study to show thyself approved unto God, a workman that needs not to be ashamed (2 Tim 2:15).

What Christ-like deed have you done?

____

____

Why do you call me Lord, Lord and not do the things that I say (Luke 6:46)?

Which temptations have you overcome?

____

____

Blessed is the man that endures temptation: for when he is tried, he shall receive the crown of life (James 1:12).

Which temptations have you yield to?

____

____

If we confess our sins, he is faithful and just to forgive us our sins, and to cleanse us from all unrighteousness (I John 1:9).

CHAPTER
FORTY-FIVE

MORE THAN
A CONQUEROR

But the apostle Paul not only got out of the jail; he won the jailer to his belief in Jesus Christ and baptized him and his family before daybreak.

I am talking about an influence that goes far beyond merely contriving to get people to do what you want them to do. I am talking about an influence that can make people what you want them to be.

The world knows many conquerors. These are people who, with brute force, shrewd cunning, wealth, or high position can get people to do what they want them to do. But the Bible says through Jesus Christ we can be "more than conquerors" (Romans 8:37). The jailer at Philippi beat Paul and locked him in stocks in a dungeon. Now a conqueror might be rescued or even break out. He might even take the jailer captive. But the apostle Paul not only got out of the jail; he won the jailer to his belief in Jesus Christ and baptized him and his family before daybreak. He did not capture his oppressor, he converted him.

Ordinary people can exert extraordinary influence

The essence of Christianity has been the strange but powerful influence of ordinary people upon all that their lives touched. "Now when the congregation was broken up, many of the Jews and religious proselytes followed Paul and Barnabas: who, speaking to them, persuaded them to continue in the grace of God" (Acts 13:43). Men were persuaded to follow Paul and Barnabas despite the fear of persecution.

The dynamic influence of Apollos enabled him to convince Jews to believe in the Jesus Christ they had crucified. "For he mightily convinced the Jews, and that publicly, showing by the scriptures that Jesus was Christ" (Acts 18:28).

When Paul was dragged in chains to Rome, you would never have dreamed that the prisoner could have had any effect upon the pompous Romans. Yet scripture records that he "persuaded them concerning Jesus" (Acts 28:23). With Jesus Christ in his heart, the prisoner can persuade his captors. The lowest employee can influence the president of his company. The most uneducated man can convert the scholar.

Most people are losers when it comes to influencing other people. The reason is obvious. They depend upon things like their power, their money, their position, their fussing, nagging, or pouting. Here's a wife who wants to influence her husband. She childishly pouts when she does not get what she wants, threatens him, or tries in some sort of way to punish him. Inevitably she fails.

People do not like to be bullied around. We often get frustrated because the only thing we know to do to influence other people is to tell them what we think they should do, argue with them or nag.

With Jesus Christ in the heart, we have the greatest forces ever known for influencing people.

Galatians 1:15, 16 says, "it pleased God . . . to reveal his Son in me." It is God's will that Jesus Christ should come to live in your heart. This enables you to reach out to others, reveal Christ and influence them. Claim the treasures of influence. It is yours. Through you God wills to work these powerful forces to change other people: love, example and wisdom.

My Daily Journal

On what date did you read this lesson ?_______

Study to show thyself approved unto God, a workman that needs not to be ashamed (2 Tim 2:15).

What Christ-like deed have you done?

____

____

Why do you call me Lord, Lord and not do the things that I say (Luke 6:46)?

Which temptations have you overcome?

____

____

Blessed is the man that endures temptation: for when he is tried, he shall receive the crown of life (James 1:12).

Which temptations have you yield to?

____

____

If we confess our sins, he is faithful and just to forgive us our sins, and to cleanse us from all unrighteousness (I John 1:9).

CHAPTER
FORTY-SIX

POSSESSING EARTH'S MOST POWERFUL FORCE

**With Jesus Christ in your heart, you have
the power to love unlovable people.**

With Christ in your heart you possess the most potent power on earth—love. The great apostle Paul declared, "The love of God is shed abroad in our hearts by the Holy Ghost which is given unto us" (Romans 5:5). This means you possess the power to love; to love your mate, your parents, your children, your friends and your enemies. You say, "Only God could love somebody acting like they are." That is true. But the miracle is that God can love them through you—"The love of God is shed abroad in our hearts by the Holy Ghost which is given unto us" (Romans 5:5).

His love is a potent force in your life. Virgil said, "Love conquers all."

William Penn said, "Force may subdue, but love gains."

Daniel A. Polling said, "Hate cannot destroy hate, but love can and does."

The *North Ireland Ulster Post* wrote about the

power of love when it said, "Money will buy a fine dog, but only love will make him wag his tail."

The English clergyman Caleb C. Colton said, "The plainest man that can convince a woman that he is really in love with her, has done more to make her in love with him than the handsomest man, if he can produce no such conviction. For the love of woman is a shoot, not a seed, and flourishes most vigorously only when engrafted on that love which is rooted in the breast of another."

The Roman poet Terence said, "It is possible that a man can be so changed by love as hardly to be recognized as the same person."

Dale Carnegie, the author of *How to Win Friends and Influence People,* says the key is to think in terms of other people's interest instead of your own. Talk about other people, not yourself. Work to serve other people, not yourself. You could reduce *How to Win Friends and Influence People* to one word—love.

God loves through human hearts

God is love. When He comes to live in your body the bondage of self-centered egotism is broken. It becomes natural to bear the fruit of the Spirit—love. It becomes natural to think of other people instead of yourself, to talk about other people instead of yourself, to serve other people instead of yourself.

Jesus Christ prayed, "that the love wherewith you have loved me may be in them, and I in them" (John 17:26). It is the will of God that Jesus Christ should live in our bodies and that with His entrance into our hearts, the greatest love in the universe becomes ours.

The scripture says the fruit of the Holy Spirit is

love (Galatians 5:22). Love is not something you work up. True love is a dynamic result of the Holy Spirit dwelling in your heart. Jesus Christ not only said, "love thy neighbor" (Matthew 19:19), He also imparts the power to do it.

The Bible declares, "Many waters cannot quench love" (Solomon's Song 8:7). Love is a fire that cannot be put out by many waters. It is a powerful force.

Jesus Christ said, "'And I, if I be lifted up from the earth, will draw all men unto me.' This he said, signifying what death he should die" (John 12:32-33). Christ said, "If I love the world enough to give my life for them I will draw all men." Everyone is drawn to the cross because of its unselfish love. All men may not come to follow Christ, but all men will be drawn by His cross. Love—it is the explosive power of God's affection.

Washington pardoned a murderer

Walter D. Cavert, in his book *Ours Is The Faith,* tells a story of a Baptist minister named Peter Miller. During the American Revolution he pastored a church in Ephrata, Pennsylvania: Among the townsfolk there was one villager who was conspicuous because of his scorn for religion and Rev. Miller. This troublemaker had been convicted of treason and sentenced to die.

Cavert relates that the minister walked sixty miles to plead with George Washington to pardon the man. The general shook his head and regretfully replied that he was sorry he could not grant the request to spare Miller's friend. To this Miller quietly replied, "My friend! He's my worst enemy." The amazed General Washington exclaimed, "What! You've walked all this distance to save an enemy? Then how can I do other than pardon him!"

Never underestimate the power of love. It can change the hearts of generals.

Love transforms a prostitute

Hosea loved and married a woman who did not return his love. She ran around with other men. His wife viciously humiliated the man who loved her before the world. She even had children by other men. She further disgraced the name of the man that had chosen her by selling her body as a prostitute.

Hosea could have walked off and left her saying, "Well, I did everything I could. She's just a no-good woman. I'm the innocent party. I think we would both be happier if I just left her and divorced her."

The years passed; his wife grows old. Her body loses its attractiveness. No man will pay the price for her body. So like all aged prostitutes she is sold as a slave.

The best she can hope for is a kindly field master. See her standing on the auction block listening to the barking of the auctioneer. She is being sold like a cow. Her hair is streaming down her face and beneath it wet tears moisten her cheek.

She never thought it would end like this. Worse than the humiliation of being sold is the humiliation that nobody wants her anymore. But then there's a voice! It sounds vaguely familiar. She brushes back the hair from her face and looks up through the teary eyes. It can't be! But it is! It's Hosea, her husband. He has come to pay the price for her freedom? He wants her? Hosea buys her freedom, puts his arms around her and takes her home. See that old couple walking off together, there goes the power of love.

Any married person can love their mate when the honeymoon is going fine. But in the midst of family crisis, when you look at your mate and say, "Only God could love someone acting like this," it becomes humanly impossible to love. But with the Lord Jesus living inside your body, you can say, "Lord I can't love anyone acting like this, but you can. I am going to trust you to shed your love abroad through my heart." Then the love of the Winner within you "is shed abroad in your hearts by the Holy Ghost" (Romans 15:5).

In my early ministry I held a crusade on the island of Jamaica. The biggest problem at the time was a domestic one. About ninety percent of the couples on the island were not married. They merely cohabited.

There was such poverty that the women had no alternative. The fathers could not afford to keep caring for the daughter. The girl, herself, could not find work to support herself in those days; so, when a man offered to feed her and care for her if she would live with him, it was that or starvation.

One of the ladies who was converted to Jesus Christ while we were there went home and tried to tell the man she had lived with, and raised a half dozen children by, that Jesus Christ had come into her heart, and furthermore that Jesus did not want them living together without being married. The man responded angrily. A short while later he came in drunk one evening, outraged that his wife had moved into a back room and would not sleep with him after her conversion. He kicked the door down and beat her severely.

But she wrote, "I will not compromise, even if he kills me." She stayed with him and loved him despite his brutality.

One of the happiest letters that I have ever received came a few months later when love triumphed and her husband received Christ and they were married.

With Jesus Christ in your heart, you have the power to love unlovable people and through loving them to change them. Never underestimate that dynamic force within your heart as a Christian.

The Winner within you can love unlovable people. You can get rid of your anger, bitterness and hatred by allowing Christ to shed His love through your heart.

My Daily Journal

On what date did you read this lesson ?_______
Study to show thyself approved unto God, a workman that needs not to be ashamed (2 Tim 2:15).

What Christ-like deed have you done?

____

____

Why do you call me Lord, Lord and not do the things that I say (Luke 6:46)?

Which temptations have you overcome?

____

____

Blessed is the man that endures temptation: for when he is tried, he shall receive the crown of life (James 1:12).

Which temptations have you yield to?

____

____

If we confess our sins, he is faithful and just to forgive us our sins, and to cleanse us from all unrighteousness (I John 1:9).

CHAPTER
FORTY-SEVEN

SHOWING OTHERS HOW TO WIN

**When God wanted to change the world,
He did not send an army or an edict,
but an example.**

"You were a good example to me when I really needed it. I just want to thank you for being what I desperately needed" are words that constitute one of the greatest rewards a person can receive. Through an exemplary life we can affect others and win this kind of appreciation. The word of God underscores the importance of this when it says, "Be you an example" (I Timothy 4:12).

The secret of changing other people is in first being changed yourself, and the secret of being changed yourself is to allow Jesus Christ to live His life in your body.

Jesus Christ, the greatest influencer of men, set others a perfect example. "I have given an example that you should walk therein" (John 13:15). Even Judas declared, after he betrayed Jesus, he had betrayed "innocent" blood: "Then Judas, which had betrayed him, when he saw that he was condemned, repented himself, and brought again the thirty pieces of silver to the chief priests and elders, saying, I have sinned in that I have betrayed the innocent blood'" (Matthew 27:3-4). Judas had no one to blame but himself. Jesus had lived an "innocent" life before him.

Albert Einstein's Theory of Influence

Albert Einstein, the great scientist, not only told us the secret of nuclear power, but also told us of the power to influence other human beings. "I am absolutely convinced that no wealth in the world can help humanity forward even in the hands of the most devoted worker in this cause. The example of great and pure individuals is the one thing that can lead us to noble thoughts and deeds. Money only appeals to selfishness and irresistibly invites abuse. Can anyone imagine Moses, Jesus, or Gandhi armed with the moneybags of Carnegie?"

When Einstein went to Princeton University he said, "I am only coming to Princeton to do research, not to teach. There's too much education altogether, especially in American schools. The only rational way of educating is to be an example—if one can't help it a warning example."

The old adage "If you can't do it, teach it" is not confined to the classroom. So much of what passes off as instruction is only the frustrated nagging of people trying to get other people to behave in a way they do not behave themselves.

Thomas Fuller said, "A father that whips his son

for swearing, and swore himself whilst he whipped him did more harm by his example than good by his correction."

Oliver Goldsmith, the English novelist, said, "People seldom improve when they have no model but themselves to copy after." No amount of effort will change people unless there is some example given them.

Francis Quarles said, "In early life I had nearly been betrayed into the principles of infidelity; but there was one argument in favor of Christianity that I could not refute, and that was the consistent character and example of my father. You canst not rebuke in children what they see practiced in thee. Such as is thy behaviour before thy children's faces, such is their's behind thy back."

The apostle Paul was the most influential Christian who ever lived. His power was "Christ lives in me." His method was telling people, "We . . . make ourselves an example unto you to follow us" (II Thessalonians 3:9). "For yourselves know how you ought to follow us: for we behaved not ourselves disorderly among you" (II Thessalonians 3:7).

Adam Swetchine said, "We reform others unconsciously, when we walk uprightly."

When God wanted to change the world, He did not send an army or an edict, but an example. Jesus Christ came in the form of a man and said, "I have left you an example that you should walk therein." Heaven knows this is the key to changing other people. May heaven help us to understand it.

My Daily Journal

On what date did you read this lesson ?_________

Study to show thyself approved unto God, a workman that needs not to be ashamed (2 Tim 2:15).

What Christ-like deed have you done?

____

____

Why do you call me Lord, Lord and not do the things that I say (Luke 6:46)?

Which temptations have you overcome?

____

____

Blessed is the man that endures temptation: for when he is tried, he shall receive the crown of life (James 1:12).

Which temptations have you yield to?

____

____

If we confess our sins, he is faithful and just to forgive us our sins, and to cleanse us from all unrighteousness (I John 1:9).

**CHAPTER
FORTY-EIGHT**

OVERCOME YOUR PAST DEFEATS

**Don't believe your difficulties.
Ignore your own weakness. The
same God that carried Moses through
a sea of difficulty will do the same for you.**

Moses wrote his name in history. He defied the entire nation of Egypt and led a half-million slaves to freedom. But it would never have happened if he had not made the great discovery of God's power.

Moses was educated, wise and mighty in word and deed. In fact, that was the problem. He was too strong. Not strong enough to succeed. But too strong to quit trying to win in his own power.

When God called him to lead the Jewish captives to freedom, he went out and hit an Egyptian. The blow was mighty enough to kill the Egyptian, but it gained Moses nothing. The Jews would not even cooperate in their own deliverance. A despondent, defeated Moses limped off bewildered: "For he supposed his brethren would have understood how that God by his hand would deliver them" (Acts 7:25). By Moses' hand? So he thought.

The Prince of Egypt
discovered the secret

Forty years later God called Moses, "'Come now therefore, and I will send thee unto Pharaoh, that you may bring forth my people the children of Israel out of Egypt.' And Moses said unto God, 'Who am I, that I should go unto Pharaoh, and that I should bring forth the children of Israel out of Egypt?' And he said, 'Certainly I will be with thee'" (Exodus 3:10-12).

That is it! Moses has discovered the secret! It does not matter that he is too weak. God is going to be with him. What about failure? Why, God never fails.

Moses is off and running. Single-handed he defies the nation of Egypt. God is with him. He escapes the entrapment of the Egyptian army and leads his nation to freedom without the power of military weapons. God's power is his strength.

If the power of God can do that through one defeated quitter, can't the same power overcome your difficulties? Face facts: "For with God nothing shall be impossible" (Luke 1:37).

Don't believe your difficulties. Ignore your own weakness. The same God that carried Moses through a sea of difficulty will do the same for you. Declare it with Micah, "I am full of power by the Spirit of the Lord."

My Daily Journal

On what date did you read this lesson ?_________

Study to show thyself approved unto God, a workman that needs not to be ashamed (2 Tim 2:15).

What Christ-like deed have you done?

____

____

Why do you call me Lord, Lord and not do the things that I say (Luke 6:46)?

Which temptations have you overcome?

____

____

Blessed is the man that endures temptation: for when he is tried, he shall receive the crown of life (James 1:12).

Which temptations have you yield to?

____

____

If we confess our sins, he is faithful and just to forgive us our sins, and to cleanse us from all unrighteousness (I John 1:9).

CHAPTER
FORTY-NINE

EXPERIENCE UNSPEAKABLE JOY

*"Joy is the echo of
God's life within us."
—Joseph Marmion*

Jay Gould, the famous multimillionaire, said, "I suppose I am the most miserable man on earth."

Marilyn Monroe became a world-famous sex symbol. She said, "I hate sex," and killed herself.

Alexander the Great conquered most of the known world. Then he sat down and cried because he was to conquer no more nations.

Voltaire, the French atheist, wrote, "I wish I had never been born."

Elizabeth I reigned over the empire on which "the sun never sets." Her wardrobe held ten-thousand dresses. Yet, she died frantically crying for another "inch of time."

They sang their way
through suffering

Clement of Alexandria, a follower of Christ in the

days of martyrdom, said Jesus "has turned all of our sunsets into sunrises!" Those early Christians, though broke, despised and rejected, shouted, "Glory to God!" and sang their way to death during the martyrdoms in Rome. Despite all their sufferings, the apostle Peter declared those early Christians "rejoiced with joy unspeakable" (I Peter 1:8). The human tongue is not capable of speaking the joy Christ brings to the heart of man.

What a contrast between the futile search for joy in selfish indulgences compared to the fantastic joy Jesus Christ imparts.

Scripture declares the Spirit of Christ lives within you to produce the fruit of joy: "But the fruit of the Spirit is love, joy, peace, longsuffering, gentleness, goodness, faith" (Galatians 5:22).

Through Jesus Christ, you can possess great joy, "for God had made them rejoice with great joy" (Nehemiah 12:43). It is a joy no one can ever take away: "Your heart shall rejoice, and your joy no man takes from you" (John 16:22). You can actually have the "God of hope fill you with all joy" (Romans 15:13). You can "rejoice with joy unspeakable" (I Peter 1:8). You can declare to God, "You shall make me full of joy" (Acts 2:28).

My Daily Journal

On what date did you read this lesson ?_______

Study to show thyself approved unto God, a workman that needs not to be ashamed (2 Tim 2:15).

What Christ-like deed have you done?

____

____

Why do you call me Lord, Lord and not do the things that I say (Luke 6:46)?

Which temptations have you overcome?

____

____

Blessed is the man that endures temptation: for when he is tried, he shall receive the crown of life (James 1:12).

Which temptations have you yield to?

____

____

If we confess our sins, he is faithful and just to forgive us our sins, and to cleanse us from all unrighteousness (I John 1:9).

CHAPTER FIFTY

JOY IS THE ECHO OF GOD'S LIFE IN MAN'S SOUL

When God by His Spirit comes to live inside man, joy is produced as naturally as an orange tree bears oranges.

Paul wrote, "For the kingdom of God is . . . joy in the Holy Ghost" (Romans 14:17). The Christians in Thessalonica "received the word in much affliction with joy of the Holy Ghost" (I Thessalonians 1:6). Outside there was much affliction, but inside there was compensation, the joy of the Holy Ghost. As Joseph Marmion said, "Joy is the echo of God's life within us."

When the apostle John wrote of his great concern for other Christians, he stated, "And these things write we unto you, that your joy may be full" (I John 1:4). There is no sense in an unhappy life and there is no fruit from an unhappy Christian. Joy is essential.

Once, when recommending the benefits of Jesus Christ, a lady told me, "If it would make me as miserable as my friends that go to that church, I couldn't stand it."

R. W. Dale said, "We asks God to forgive us for our evil thoughts and evil temper, but rarely, if ever, asks him to forgive us for our sadness."

The Gospel of Jesus Christ is capable of converting mankind and solving all the other problems, but it is impossible to recommend it when there is a lack of joy in those that profess it. That is exactly the whole point the Bible makes on joy. It is not outside, but within. Galatians 5:22 says, "the fruit of the Spirit is . . . joy." When God by His Spirit comes to live inside man, joy is produced as naturally as an orange tree bears oranges. The joy comes from within.

Joy is more important than life itself

Paul valued joy greater than he valued his own life. As he saw his inevitable execution drawing near, he said, "And now, behold, I go bound in the spirit unto Jerusalem, not knowing the things that shall befall me there: Save that the Holy Ghost witnesses in every city, saying that bonds and afflictions abide me. But none of these things move me, neither count I my life dear unto myself, so that I might finish my course with joy, and the ministry, which I have received of the Lord Jesus, to testify the gospel of the grace of God" (Acts 20:22-24). Paul was not at all concerned with escaping death. He was concerned with going through all of his suffering "with joy."

I once asked the outstanding Christian author and songwriter, Lee Fisher, how he felt. Lee grinned and replied, "Jesus makes me feel so good, I feel good even when I don't feel good!" Jesus Christ puts a joy within the heart of man that overcomes all outward circumstances and all physical sufferings.

My Daily Journal

On what date did you read this lesson ?___________
Study to show thyself approved unto God, a workman that needs not to be ashamed (2 Tim 2:15).

What Christ-like deed have you done?
____

____
Why do you call me Lord, Lord and not do the things that I say (Luke 6:46)?

Which temptations have you overcome?
____

____
Blessed is the man that endures temptation: for when he is tried, he shall receive the crown of life (James 1:12).

Which temptations have you yield to?
____

____
If we confess our sins, he is faithful and just to forgive us our sins, and to cleanse us from all unrighteousness (I John 1:9).

CHAPTER
FIFTY-ONE

WIN OVER HORRIBLE HANDICAPS

"Your success and happiness lie in you. External conditions are the accidents of life. Joy is the holy fire that keeps our purpose warm and our intelligence aglow. Resolve to keep happy and your joy in you shall form an invincible host against difficulty."
—Helen Keller

You can experience a winning life despite considerable handicaps. If you have some disability or handicap, you will be excited by the story of Helen Adams Keller. Born in 1880, she was a blind deaf-mute. Her education and training represents the most extraordinary accomplishment ever made in the education of persons so handicapped. Her problems were the result of a severe illness that struck her at the age of nineteen months. She was deprived of sight and hearing and soon became mute.

Her education began on March 2, 1887, with Anne Mansfield Sullivan as her instructor. Miss Keller not only learned to read, write and talk, but she entered Radcliffe College in 1900 and graduated cum laude in 1904.

Success and happiness
are within you

Among her many books and articles were: *Optimism* (1903), *Out of the Dark* (1913), *My Religion* (1927), *Peace at Eventide* (1932) and *Let Us Have Faith* (1940). Before her passing in 1968, Miss Keller left her formula for joy. She said, "Your success and happiness lie in you. External conditions are the accidents of life. Joy is the holy fire that keeps our purpose warm and our intelligence aglow. Resolve to keep happy and your joy in you shall form an invincible host against difficulty."

If there is one thing that the joyful life of Helen Keller teaches us, it is this, "success has nothing to do with outward circumstances."

My Daily Journal

On what date did you read this lesson ?________

Study to show thyself approved unto God, a workman that needs not to be ashamed (2 Tim 2:15).

What Christ-like deed have you done?

____

____

Why do you call me Lord, Lord and not do the things that I say (Luke 6:46)?

Which temptations have you overcome?

____

____

Blessed is the man that endures temptation: for when he is tried, he shall receive the crown of life (James 1:12).

Which temptations have you yield to?

____

____

If we confess our sins, he is faithful and just to forgive us our sins, and to cleanse us from all unrighteousness (I John 1:9).

CHAPTER
FIFTY-TWO

SATISFACTION THAT NEVER ENDS

Don't make the mistake of thinking that you must have to have the right mate, the right job, the right amount of money, or the right anything to be happy. Jesus Christ can override the circumstances and flood your life with satisfaction.

A dejected Samaritan woman met Jesus, discovered the secret of joy and went out to turn her city upside down.

When Jesus departed from Judea on His way to Galilee, He stopped at the city of Sychar to drink water from Jacob's well and rest. A woman of Samaria came there to draw water and Jesus asked her for a drink. The woman questioned, "How is it that you, being a Jew, asks drink of me, which am a woman of Samaria? for the Jews have no dealings with the Samaritans" (John 4:9). Jesus replied, "If you knew the gift of God, and who it is that says to thee, Give me to drink; you would have asked of him, and he would have given thee living water" (John 4:10).

Christ then told her, "Whosoever drinks of this water shall thirst again: But whosoever drinks of the water that I shall give him shall never thirst; but the water that I shall give him shall be in him a well of water springing up into everlasting life" (John 4:13-14). When the woman heard about water that could forever end dissatisfaction, she said, "Sir, give me this water" (John 4:15).

As a young girl, I can picture her playing with her dolls and thinking, "When I grow up, I am going to have a little baby of my own and I am going to be so happy." Finally, that time came. She is getting married. I see her approaching the wedding with great excitement. She thinks, "At last I am going to have the happiness that I have waited for from youth." But something didn't work out. The marriage was broken. She tries again. There is a second marriage. There's not quite as much excitement this time, but still she thinks, "This is the right man. This time I'm going to be happy."

But something happened to that second marriage also and likewise to the third, the fourth and the fifth. Now she is living, Jesus said, with a man who was not her husband.

This woman is a picture of many disappointed people. They believe if they can ever get the outward circumstances arranged properly, they will have the joy they desire. If they can just have the right husband, the right house, the right clothes, the right automobile, the right neighbors, the right job, etc., everything is going to be wonderful. If men live long enough, they all come to the same disillusionment that raged within this woman's breast. But Jesus said, speaking of His Spirit, "whosoever drinks of the water that I shall give him shall never thirst."

That day the woman discovered the Messiah and with Him the key to joy—God within you. She went running down the streets calling the people of her city to come and see Jesus and "many of the Samaritans of that city believed in him because of this woman's testimony" (John 4:39). Before the day was over her joy turned the city to the Lord.

Don't make the mistake of thinking that you must have the right mate, the right job, the right amount of money, or the right anything to be happy. Jesus Christ can override the circumstances and flood your life with satisfaction. The key is within you.

My Daily Journal

On what date did you read this lesson ?________
Study to show thyself approved unto God, a workman that needs not to be ashamed (2 Tim 2:15).

What Christ-like deed have you done?

____

____

Why do you call me Lord, Lord and not do the things that I say (Luke 6:46)?

Which temptations have you overcome?

____

Blessed is the man that endures temptation: for when he is tried, he shall receive the crown of life (James 1:12).

Which temptations have you yield to?

____

If we confess our sins, he is faithful and just to forgive us our sins, and to cleanse us from all unrighteousness (I John 1:9).

CHAPTER
FIFTY-THREE

EXPERIENCE
ENDLESS ENTHUSIASM

Everyone that allows the Winner within to fill them, and control them, certainly is enthusiastic. And they stay enthusiastic.

The root meaning of the word "enthusiasm" is "God filled." Everybody that is called enthusiastic is not necessarily "God filled." But everyone that allows the Winner within to fill them, or control them, certainly is enthusiastic. And they stay enthusiastic. A. L. Williams said, "Most people can stay excited for two or three months. A few people can stay excited for two or three years. But a Winner will stay excited for twenty or thirty years—or as long as it takes to win. If you're a leader of other people, you've got to set an example of being excited. People won't follow a dull, disillusioned, frustrated crybaby. If you're excited, you draw people like a magnet. Everyone wants to know what you're feeling. They all want to experience the kind of excitement you have."[6]

Nothing is more exciting than Jesus, who loved us enough to die for us and then rose from the dead.

When the apostle Peter heard Mary Magdalene and Joanna and Mary telling about Jesus rising from the dead, he got excited: "Then arose Peter, and ran unto the sepulchre." Peter was no boy, but he ran to see the empty tomb and then ran to tell the world Jesus had risen" (Luke 24:10-12).

Focus on the Christ living within you. Claim His enthusiasm. He will fill you with an explosive zest for living.

My Daily Journal

On what date did you read this lesson ? _______
Study to show thyself approved unto God, a workman that needs not to be ashamed (2 Tim 2:15).

What Christ-like deed have you done?

____

____

Why do you call me Lord, Lord and not do the things that I say (Luke 6:46)?

Which temptations have you overcome?

____

____

Blessed is the man that endures temptation: for when he is tried, he shall receive the crown of life (James 1:12).

Which temptations have you yield to?

____

____

If we confess our sins, he is faithful and just to forgive us our sins, and to cleanse us from all unrighteousness (I John 1:9).

CHAPTER
FIFTY-FOUR

WINNERS LIVE
IN ANOTHER WORLD

*It is great to go to heaven when you die,
but there is something better—to
go to heaven before you die!*

It is great to go to heaven when you die, but there is something better—to go to heaven before you die! The Bible says God has "made us to sit in heavenly places in Christ." The thing that makes heaven is Jesus' presence and you can have that here and now! Psalm 16:11 says, "in thy presence is fullness of joy."

They often beat the apostle Paul, stoned him and put him in prison. Did he write and asks people to please pray for him because he "couldn't hold out much longer" or declare, "I don't know why God is letting me suffer like this"? No, Paul spent his time in the dungeons writing to cheer up people on the outside. He wrote about "love, peace, and joy." He dragged his chains across the page and made them rattle like the joy bells of heaven.

Paul had no material wealth. Stocks and bonds? The only stocks he knew were those that shackled his neck; and the only bonds he knew were those that were binding his wrists; but he had Jesus Christ in his heart. Because of the presence of Jesus he could say, "I have learned, in whatsoever state I am, therewith to be content" (Philippians 4:11). Jails don't phase that kind of joy.

The world thought Paul was crazy. They called him "mad." But they did not know what he had on the inside. He walked around his cell grinning and talking about joy. Appearances were certainly deceiving. You would have never dreamed that in Paul's earthen vessel was the treasure of God's presence.

When Bertha Adams went begging for food among her West Palm Beach neighbors, she wore clothes from the Salvation Army and only weighed fifty pounds. No one believed her when she contended she was "a wealthy woman," but when the seventy-one-year-old widow passed away at the end of March, 1975, they found she had over a million dollars in stocks and $850 in cash.

One neighbor, Mrs. Odell Edwards, said, "She came to my back door and begged me for food. She always used to tell me that she was no poor woman." Appearances sure can be deceiving. There are many people who appear frail and poor, but they actually possess the most priceless treasure—Christ is inside their bodies.

The man with half a head

In east Texas an old man called "the man with half a head," told me why he felt sorry for other people. "Sure, cancer has eaten up half my head (one eye, a cheekbone, half his jaw, and a large part of his brains was gone)," he said, "but I've got Jesus in my heart. Folks come out here from town and look at me with pity, and all the while I am pitying them because they don't have Jesus. Soon I am going to get me a new head, but until then, Jesus is in my heart, and I'm so happy I can hardly stand it." When I left his little shotgun house and drove away on that dusty Texas road, all doubt was forever gone about the joy God's presence could bring, even to a dying man with half of a head.

My Daily Journal

On what date did you read this lesson ? _________
Study to show thyself approved unto God, a workman that needs not to be ashamed (2 Tim 2:15).

What Christ-like deed have you done?

____

____

Why do you call me Lord, Lord and not do the things that I say (Luke 6:46)?

Which temptations have you overcome?

____

____

Blessed is the man that endures temptation: for when he is tried, he shall receive the crown of life (James 1:12).

Which temptations have you yield to?

____

____

If we confess our sins, he is faithful and just to forgive us our sins, and to cleanse us from all unrighteousness (I John 1:9).

CHAPTER
FIFTY-FIVE

FACE THE FUTURE WITH UNSHAKABLE ASSURANCE

*He is already in us, the dawn of the coming day.
We are in vital contact with our destiny, that
marvelous destiny of companionship with
God throughout the ages. We have in this
experience the hope of it. Christ is in us
the hope of the glory yet to be revealed.*
—*Gregory Mantle*

One day when I finished speaking south of New Orleans, a big burly Frenchman grabbed me by the arm and said, "Come with me." I said, "Where are we going?" He replied, "Man, you are going to get the blessing of your life." I said, "Well, that's wonderful, but where are we going to get it?" He answered with a big smile, "To a cemetery."

When we reached the burial ground, he jumped out; and with an exuberance that was excessive even for a Frenchman, he said, "Look at that!" And there it was. He pointed to a grave, like all of those in the marshes of south Louisiana, above ground. But this one was standing straight up. I said, "Why did they prepare the grave like that?" He said, "That was his last request, that he be buried standing up." When they asked him why, he told them because he was a Christian. They said a lot of Christians had been buried laying down, and they couldn't understand why he had to be different. He told them he had something more to look forward to than laying down to rest, that he wanted to be "standing and ready when the Lord Jesus came."

The God-given assurance you are going to heaven

There are only two kinds of people in the world, those with an assurance of heaven and those waiting for the undertaker. Somebody said they didn't know why people drank and took drugs so much. I sure understand it. If I didn't have anything to look forward to but the mortician backing up to my house, loading me up, dressing me and putting me in the ground, I'd stay drunk. I'd stay on drugs. It's not a drug problem, it's a death problem. But when Christ Jesus comes into our heart, He give us logical, valid, substantial proof of life beyond the grave.

That proof that God is going to give us an eternal home in heaven is the gift He has already given—His life within us. Paul said, "Being confident of this very thing, that he which hath begun a good work in you will perform it until the day of Jesus Christ!" (Philippians 1:6).

Paul knew that God had already begun a good

work, for Christ had come into him. This was his assurance that God would complete that work on the day Christ comes to take him to heaven. If God could not finish a man's redemption, why would He have ever started it?

Scripture declared we have already received the down payment on heaven. "Who (God) hath . . . given the earnest of the Spirit in our hearts" (II Corinthians 1:22). When a man puts up one-third earnest money on a house, it is pretty good indication that he intends to complete the transaction. Christ within us is God's earnest: a certain assurance of heaven to come.

God's work within us makes us children of God and gives us every right to the inheritance of God-heaven! "The Spirit itself bears witness with our spirit, that we are the children of God: And if children, then heirs; heirs of God, and joint-heirs with Christ; if so be that we suffer with him, that we may be also glorified together" (Romans 8:16-17).

The hope is within us

Gregory Mantle, a great minister, said, "Our union with our risen Lord is of such a character that we become partakers of His very nature; drawing our spiritual life from His Spirit; our mental vigor from His mind; our physical strength from His risen body; and our power for service from His omnipotence. He is already in us, the dawn of the coming day. We are in vital contact with our destiny, that marvelous destiny of companionship with God throughout the ages. We have in this experience the hope of it. Christ is in us the hope of the glory yet to be revealed.

"Blessed   are   the   sons   of   God, They are bought with Christ's own blood; One with

God, with Jesus one; Glory is in them begun."[7]

The power of the resurrection is already working within us. "But if the Spirit of him that raised up Jesus from the dead dwell in you, he that raised up Christ from the dead shall also quicken your mortal bodies by his Spirit that dwells in you" (Romans 8:11). The presence of Jesus within us gives us the joyful expectancy. "Weeping may endure for a night, but joy comes in the morning" (Psalms 30:5).

The joy of Jesus is the only adequate joy. None of the others last long enough. "The triumphing of the wicked is short, and the joy of the hypocrite but for a moment?" (Job 20:5). The wicked have fun, but death suddenly ends it.

With Jesus in our hearts we possess the overflowing joy that sings:

"I'm gwine to heaven
    On eagle's wing;
All don't see me,
    Is goin to hear me sing."

Samuel Dickey Gordon said, "Joy has its springs deep down inside and that spring never runs dry, no matter what happens. Only Jesus gives that joy. He had joy, singing its music within, even under the shadow of the cross. It is an unknown word, except as He has sway within."

My Daily Journal

On what date did you read this lesson ?_______

Study to show thyself approved unto God, a workman that needs not to be ashamed (2 Tim 2:15).

What Christ-like deed have you done?

____

____

Why do you call me Lord, Lord and not do the things that I say (Luke 6:46)?

Which temptations have you overcome?

____

____

Blessed is the man that endures temptation: for when he is tried, he shall receive the crown of life (James 1:12).

Which temptations have you yield to?

____

____

If we confess our sins, he is faithful and just to forgive us our sins, and to cleanse us from all unrighteousness (I John 1:9).

CHAPTER
FIFTY-SIX

START YOUR WINNING LIFE TODAY

"Let me henceforth seat Christ, my Redeemer and
my King, on the very throne of my heart, and then
keep every gate of my body and every avenue
of my mind as all not any more mine but His."
—Dr. Alexander Whyte

To enjoy the new life of the Winner, you must first
give up the life of the loser. Jesus said, "Take up a
cross"—or give up your life. Paul said, "I die daily."

Gregory Mantle explains the key in his comment
on II Corinthians 5:14-15: "'We thus judge, that one
died for all, therefore all died; and he died for all, that
they that live should no longer live unto themselves,
but unto him who for their sakes died and rose again.'
The question in every life is, Who is on the throne?
The power ruling within determines the character of
the life manifested, for a throne implies a king. "Are
we living unto ourselves, or unto Him who for our
sakes died and rose again?

Charles Wesley's hymn put it this way:

'More of Thy life and more I have,
As the old Adam dies;
Bury me, Savior, in Thy grave,
That I with Thee may rise.'

Give up your life for His

Gregory Mantle said, "There are multitudes that never differentiate, in their prayers and utterances, between Jesus as Savior and Jesus as Lord and King. He must be absolute Ruler, else the inexpressible possibilities of the Christian calling can never become actualities. There must be no more living to 'ourselves.' 'I was quite willing,' said one, 'that Jesus Christ should be King, so long as He allowed me to be Prime Minister.' In other words, 'I want to be permitted, now and again, to assert my independence; there are certain matters which I wish to decide on my own account. There is certain business in the kingdom of my being that I want to transact. But that can never be.'"[8]

Let Christ reign as King

Dr. Alexander Whyte appeals with Christians to allow the Christ within them to reign as King: "Let me henceforth seat Christ, my Redeemer and my King, on the very throne of my heart, and then keep every gate of my body and every avenue of my mind as all not any more mine but His. Let me open my eye, my ear, and my mouth, and all my members, as if, in all that, I were opening Christ's eye, Christ's ear, and Christ's mouth; and let me thrust nothing on Him, as He dwells within me, that will make Him ashamed or grieved, or that will defile or pollute Him. Yes, O Paul, I shall henceforth hold with thee that my body is the temple of Christ, and that I am not my own, but that I am bought with a paralyzing price, and must therefore, do nothing less than glorify God in my body and in my spirit, which are God's."

Allow Christ to be your all

Romaine, writing in *The Inward Cross,* says: "If Christ be not all in all, Self must still be looked upon as something great, and there will be food left for the pride of self-importance and self-sufficiency. Seek for the death of sin where you wilt, it is not to be found but in His death. Dethroned in the life by the power of the Cross of Jesus . . . sin is put to a lingering death, kept upon the Cross, dying daily."

Give up your life and let Him live through your body. Get out the old treasure map of the Bible. Read what you have in Christ. File your claim on all that is promised. Day by day you will discover the power, the riches, and the victory of the Winner within you.

My Daily Journal

On what date did you read this lesson ?_______

Study to show thyself approved unto God, a workman that needs not to be ashamed (2 Tim 2:15).

What Christ-like deed have you done?

____

____

Why do you call me Lord, Lord and not do the things that I say (Luke 6:46)?

Which temptations have you overcome?

____

____

Blessed is the man that endures temptation: for when he is tried, he shall receive the crown of life (James 1:12).

Which temptations have you yield to?

____

____

If we confess our sins, he is faithful and just to forgive us our sins, and to cleanse us from all unrighteousness (I John 1:9).

END NOTES

[1]Rev. J. Gregory Mantle, *Beyond Humiliation*,
[Moody Press Chicago].

[2]Charles G. Trumbull, *Victory in Christ*,
[The Sunday School Times, Philadelphia], pp. 9, 13.

[3]Rev. J. Gregory Mantle, *Beyond Humiliation*,
[Moody Press, Chicago], pp. 191-192.

[4]Zig Ziglar, *See You at the Top*, [Pelican, Gretna, La.], p.41.

[5]Watchman Nee, *The Normal Christian Life*,
{Witness and Testimony Publishers, London].

[6]A. L. Williams, *All You Can Do Is All You Can Do*,
[Oliver Nelson, Nashville], p. 129.

[7]Rev. J. Gregory Mantle, *Beyond Humiliation*,
[Moody Press, Chicago].

[8]Rev. J. Gregory Mantle, *Beyond Humiliation*,
[Moody Press, Chicago].